JUST
5
INGREDIENTS

LOW CALORIE

D1343012

521 856 66 2

An Hachette UK Company
www.hachette.co.uk

First published in Great Britain in 2015 by
Hamlyn, a division of Octopus Publishing Group Ltd
Endeavour House
189 Shaftesbury Avenue
London
WC2H 8JY

Some of the recipes in this book have previously been published by Hamlyn.

ISBN 978-0-60062-918-4

A CIP catalogue record for this book is available from the British Library

Printed and bound in China

10 9 8 7 6 5 4 3 2

Commissioning Editor Eleanor Maxfield
Editor Pauline Bache
Designers Jeremy Tilston, Jaz Bahra & Eoghan O'Brien
Assistant Production Manager Caroline Alberti

Standard level spoon measurement are used in all recipes.
1 tablespoon = one 15 ml spoon
1 teaspoon = one 5 ml spoon

Both imperial and metric measurements have been given in all recipes. Use one set
of measurements only and not a mixture of both.

Eggs should be medium unless otherwise stated. The Department of Health advises
that eggs should not be consumed raw. This book contains dishes made with raw or
lightly cooked eggs. It is prudent for more vulnerable people such as pregnant and
nursing mothers, invalids, the elderly, babies and young children to avoid uncooked
or lightly cooked dishes made with eggs. Once prepared these dishes should be kept
refrigerated and used promptly.

Milk should be full fat unless otherwise stated.

Ovens should be preheated to the specific temperature – if using a fan-assisted oven,
follow manufacturer's instructions for adjusting the time and the temperature.

All microwave information is based on a 650-watt oven. Follow manufacturer's
instructions for an oven with a different wattage.

This book includes dishes made with nuts and nut derivatives. It is advisable for
customers with known allergic reactions to nuts and nut derivatives and those
who may be potentially vulnerable to these allergies, such as pregnant and nursing
mothers, invalids, the elderly, babies and children, to avoid dishes made with nuts
and nut oils. It is also prudent to check the labels of pre-prepared ingredients for
the possible inclusion of nut derivatives.

JUST
5
INGREDIENTS

LOW CALORIE

MAKE LIFE SIMPLE WITH MORE THAN 100 RECIPES USING 5 INGREDIENTS OR FEWER

hamlyn

CONTENTS

INTRODUCTION

The recipes in this book have been chosen not only for their simplicity and great flavours, but also because they use just five or fewer main ingredients.

Applying a five-ingredient approach to cooking will help you create a repertoire of quick, easy, adaptable dishes, that are not only cheap and tasty but that also require little shopping and preparation. You will learn to master some basic recipes in record time and come to appreciate that cooking for yourself is a satisfying and empowering process.

This will make your life easier in three ways. First, because the recipes are straightforward there is less fiddly preparation, which will save you time. Second, you will find that shopping is simpler. How long do you really want to wander around a supermarket searching for something to cook? And third, it will save money. The five-ingredient approach will mean that you don't have a fridge full of half-used packets of strange ingredients left over from previous meals.

Unlike other five-ingredient cookbooks, you won't have hundreds of hidden added extras to stock up on. This series requires you to remember 10 storecupboard extras only – simple, easy-to-remember basics you will no doubt already have to hand.

Start by stocking up on your storecupboard 10 (see page 11). Make sure you have at least some of them at all times so that you are just five ingredients away from a decent meal.

Next, choose a recipe that suits the time you have to cook, your energy levels and your mood. Check what storecupboard ingredients you will need on the list. The five key ingredients you will need to complete the dish are clearly numbered.

One of the best ways to eat cheaply is to avoid costly processed foods. Instead, buy basic ingredients such as vegetables, rice, pasta, fish and chicken, and build your meals around these. You should also try to avoid waste and not spend money on food you don't eat and that has to be thrown away. Buy food that lasts and plan around the lifetime dates of foods. If you have a freezer, freeze the leftovers for another day.

Plan your meals for the week so you need to go shopping only once a week. When you get into the habit of doing this the ingredients for each meal will be waiting when you need them. Buy in bulk to get the best prices. Make time to shop around and compare prices in the nearest supermarket, online, your local shops and on market stalls to see which is cheapest. Stick to buying fruit and vegetables that are in season.

Not only will they be better value than exotic produce flown in from abroad but you will be reducing your food miles. Finally, don't even think about spending precious cash on a supermarket's special offer unless it is something you will actually use. Three tins of pilchards in mustard sauce for the price of one is good value only if you are going to eat them.

This book offers a range of delicious recipes that are low in calories but still high in flavour. Each recipe shows a calorie count per portion, so you will know exactly what you are eating. These are recipes for real and delicious food, not ultra-slimming meals, so they will help you maintain a healthier eating plan for life. They must be used as part of a balanced diet, with the cakes and sweet dishes eaten only as an occasional treat.

As we all know, one of the major causes of obesity is eating too many calories. Based on our relatively inactive modern-day lifestyles, most nutritionists recommend that women should aim to consume around 2,000 calories (kcal) per day, and men an amount of around 2,500. For a woman, the aim is to reduce her daily calorie intake to around 1,500 kcal while she is trying to lose weight, then settle on around 2,000 per day thereafter to maintain her new body weight. Physical activity doesn't just help us control body weight; it also helps to reduce our appetites and is known to have beneficial effects on the heart and blood that help guard against cardiovascular disease. As a general guide, adults should aim to undertake at least 30 minutes of moderate-intensity exercise, such as a brisk walk, five times a week. The 30 minutes does not have to be taken all at once: three sessions of 10 minutes are equally beneficial. Children and young people should be encouraged to take at least 60 minutes of moderate-intensity exercise every day.

Remember
Eat more fruit and vegetables, aiming for at least five portions of different fruit and vegetables a day (excluding potatoes). Eat fewer sugary foods and look out for hidden sugar. This will also help reduce your fat intake. Low-fat versions are available for most dairy products, including milk, cheese, crème fraîche,

yogurt, and even cream and butter. Choose lean cuts of meat, such as back bacon instead of streaky, and chicken breasts instead of thighs. Trim all visible fat off meat before cooking and avoid frying foods – grill or roast instead. Fish is naturally low in fat and can make tempting dishes.

Enjoy!

WEEKLY PLANNER

SUPERFOODS

MONDAY
Walnut & Banana Sunrise Smoothie (see page 34)

TUESDAY
Warm Aubergine Salad (see page 38)

WEDNESDAY
Coconut Citrus Squid (see page 152)

THURSDAY
Spinach & Ricotta Frittata (see page 114)

FRIDAY
Moroccan Grilled Sardines (see page 144)

SATURDAY
Lemon Grass Chicken (see page 116)

STORECUPBOARD 10

The only extras you will need!

1 Sugars

2 Flours

3 Oils and vinegars

4 Baking Powder

5 Salt

6 Pepper

7 Stocks

8 Onion

9 Garlic

10 Lemon and lemon juice

SUNDAY
Trout with Pesto (see page 110)

SHOPPING LIST

- 10–12 prepared baby squid, about 375 g (12 oz) including tentacles
- 12 sardines
- 12 large chicken drumsticks
- 4 trout fillets, about 200 g (7 oz) each
- 2 tablespoons capers
- 400 g (13 oz) can butter beans
- 2 tablespoons harissa
- 2 tablespoons medium curry paste
- 1 orange
- 1 banana
- 25 g (1 oz) walnut pieces
- 2 aubergines
- 4 tomatoes
- 6 limes
- 3 red chillies
- 2.5 cm (1 inch) piece of fresh root ginger
- 100 g (3½ oz) freshly grated coconut
- 200 g (7 oz) baby spinach leaves
- 6 tablespoons very finely chopped lemon grass
- 1 lemon grass stalk
- salad
- 4 tablespoons chopped parsley
- chopped coriander
- large handful of basil
- 150 ml (¼ pint) skimmed milk
- 150 g (5 oz) natural yogurt
- 4 eggs
- 50 g (2 oz) ricotta cheese
- 50 g (2 oz) Parmesan cheese

WEEKLY PLANNER

DETOX

MONDAY
Tuna & Borlotti Bean Salad (see page 56)

TUESDAY
Chicken & Vegetable Skewers (see page 76)

WEDNESDAY
Sweet Potato & Cabbage Soup (see page 84)

THURSDAY
Prawns with Tamarind & Lime (see page 86)

FRIDAY
Griddled Tuna Salad (see page 106)

SATURDAY
Chilli & Coriander Fish Parcels (see page 128)

STORECUPBOARD 10

The only extras you will need!

1 Sugars

2 Flours

3 Oils and vinegars

4 Baking Powder

5 Salt

6 Pepper

7 Stocks

8 Onion

9 Garlic

10 Lemon and lemon juice

SHOPPING LIST

- 4 chicken thighs
- 4 lean back bacon rashers
- 1 kg (2 lb) large, uncooked langoustine prawns in their shell
- 500g (1 lb) boneless, skinless chicken breasts
- 125 g (4 oz) cod, coley or haddock fillet
- 4 fresh tuna steaks, about 175 g (6 oz) each
- 400 g (13 oz) can borlotti beans
- 200 g (7 oz) can tuna in olive oil
- 2 tablespoons clear honey
- 2 tablespoons mild wholegrain mustard
- 2 teaspoons tamarind paste
- 1 red chilli
- 2 celery sticks
- 50 g (2 oz) wild rocket leaves
- 100 g (3½ oz) baby spinach leaves, roughly chopped
- 1 courgette
- 1 carrot
- 500 g (1 lb) sweet potatoes
- 500 g (1 lb) small new potatoes
- 2 parsnips
- 1 baby Savoy cabbage
- 4 cm (1½ inch) piece of fresh root ginger
- 4 limes
- 1 green chilli
- 1 spring onion
- 1 teaspoon chopped thyme
- medium bunch of coriander
- 2 teaspoons natural yogurt
- 1 egg

SUNDAY
Low-fat Lemon Chicken (see page 148)

5 FOR VEGGIES

With only 5 key ingredients, these veggie meals with satisfy vegetarians and meat eaters alike. Helping you towards your recommended 5-a-day, they are packed with vitamins and nutrients too.

Moroccan Chickpea Salad (see page 46)

Wild Mushroom Omelette (see page 70)

Vegetable Curry (see page 64)

Pepper & Walnut Papparadelle (see page 118)

Butternut Squash & Ricotta Frittata (see page 72)

5 FOR CHICKEN

Lean, quick and easily available, chicken is the perfect meat to eat when watching your weight, and it's a great base for absorbing all the flavours from your 5 ingredients.

Griddled Summer Chicken Salad (see page 98)

Seared Chicken Sandwich (see page 44)

Greek Chicken Avgolomeno (see page 82)

Fast Chicken Curry (see page 108)

Chicken with Orange & Mint (see page 142)

5 FOR FISH & SEAFOOD

While it's great, tasty source of protein, some people are intimidated at the prospect of preparing fish dishes, but with just 5 key ingredients, these dishes are so simple you'll be gaining confidence and eating in no time!

Baked Cod with Tomatoes & Olives (see page 60)

Bass with Tomato & Basil Sauce (see page 68)

Smoked Salmon Risotto (see page 120)

Swordfish with Couscous & Salsa (see page 132)

Warm Scallop Salad (see page 48)

5 FOR SUMMER SUPPERS

Summer is the time when the pressure's on to be in your best shape ever, and these light, refreshing suppers are perfect to choose for al fresco eating, and making the most of the long days.

Bean, Kabanos & Pepper Salad (see page 50)

Prosciutto & Rocket Pizza (see page 92)

Watermelon & Feta Salad (see page 52)

Chicken Teriyaki (see page 94)

Griddled Bananas with Blueberries (see page 182)

5 FOR WARMING UP

Healthy, low-calorie food doesn't mean you have to compromise at those times when comfort food is what's needed, and these warming, indulgent dishes provide winter treats, without any of the usual naughtiness.

Pumpkin & Goats' Cheese Bake (see page 66)

Bacon & White Bean Soup (see page 74)

Pepper-crusted Loin of Venison (see page 130)

Poached Peaches & Raspberries (see page 88)

Calves' Liver with Garlic Mash (see page 100)

5 FOR EASTERN FLAVOUR

Thai, Indian, Chinese and Japanese food all pack in the flavour without soaring calories and, with only 5 ingredients each in these recipes, you won't have to spend hours trailing the supermarket aisles to take your tastebuds on a journey.

Chai Teabread (see page 24)

Thai Red Pork & Bean Curry (see page 80)

Sugar & Spice Salmon (see page 138)

Lychee & Coconut Sherbet (see page 186)

Griddled Tandoori Chicken (see page 112)

SNACKS,
SALADS
& LIGHT
BITES

MAKES 2 × 300 ML (½ PINT) GLASSES

Calories per serving 89
Preparation time 2 minutes

INGREDIENTS

1	1 ripe peach, halved, pitted and chopped
2	150 g (5 oz) strawberries
3	150 g (5 oz) raspberries
4	200 ml (7 fl oz) milk
5	ice cubes

Fruity Summer Milkshakes

■ Put the peach in a blender or food processor with the strawberries and raspberries and blend to a smooth purée, scraping the mixture down from the sides of the bowl if necessary.

■ Add the milk and blend the ingredients again until the mixture is smooth and frothy. Pour the milkshake over the ice cubes in tall glasses.

MAKES 10 SLICES

Calories per serving 302
Preparation time 15 minutes, plus standing
Cooking time 1¼ hours

INGREDIENTS

1	5 chai tea bags

2	300 g (10 oz) mixed dried fruit

3	50 g (2 oz) Brazil nuts, chopped

4	50 g (2 oz) butter

5	1 egg, beaten

STORECUPBOARD

300 ml (½ pint) boiling water; 250 g (8 oz)
self-raising flour; 1 teaspoon baking powder;
150 g (5 oz) light muscovado sugar

Chai Teabread

■ Stir the tea bags into the water and
leave to stand for 10 minutes.

■ Mix together the flour, baking powder,
sugar, dried fruit and nuts in a bowl. Remove
the tea bags from the water, squeezing out
all the water. Thinly slice the butter into
the tea and stir until melted. Leave to cool
slightly. Add to the dry ingredients with the
egg and mix together well.

■ Spoon the mixture into a greased and
lined 1 kg (2 lb) or 1.3 litre (2¼ pint) loaf
tin and spread the mixture right into the
corners. Bake in a preheated oven, 160°C
(325°F), Gas Mark 3, for 1¼ hours or until
risen, firm and a skewer inserted into the
centre comes out clean. Loosen the cake
and transfer to a wire rack. Peel off the
lining paper and leave to cool. Spread
the top with Chai Cream Frosting, if liked
(see right).

FOR CHAI CREAM FROSTING

Put 50 ml (2 fl oz) milk and 3 chai tea bags in a saucepan and bring to the boil. Remove from the heat and leave until cold. Discard the tea bags, squeezing them to extract the liquid. Beat together 200 g (7 oz) cream cheese and 25 g (1 oz) very soft unsalted butter in a bowl until smooth. Beat in the flavoured milk and 75 g (3 oz) sifted icing sugar. Calories per serving 113

MAKES 12

Calories per muffin 172
Preparation time 10 minutes
Cooking time 20 minutes

INGREDIENTS

1 3 pieces stem ginger from a jar, about 50 g (2 oz), finely chopped

2 100 g (3½ oz) dried cranberries

3 1 egg

4 250 ml (8 fl oz) milk

STORECUPBOARD

150 g (5 oz) plain flour; 150 g (5 oz) self-raising flour; 1 tablespoon baking powder; 65 g (2½ oz) light muscovado sugar; 4 tablespoons vegetable oil

Cranberry Muffins

■ Line a 12-hole muffin tin with paper muffin cases. Sift the flours and baking powder into a large bowl. Stir in the sugar, ginger and cranberries until evenly distributed.

■ Beat together the egg, milk and oil in a separate bowl, then add the liquid to the flour mixture. Using a large metal spoon, gently stir the liquid into the flour, until only just combined. The mixture should look craggy, with specks of flour still visible.

■ Divide the mixture between the muffin cases, piling it up in the centre. Bake in a preheated oven, 200°C (400°F), Gas Mark 6, for 18–20 minutes, until well risen and golden. Transfer to a wire rack and serve while still slightly warm.

Calories per serving 348
Preparation time 5 minutes, plus chilling

INGREDIENTS

1	2 passion fruit
2	250 ml (8 fl oz) natural yogurt
3	4 tablespoons clear honey
4	50 g (2 oz) hazelnuts, toasted and roughly chopped
5	4 clementines, peeled and chopped into small pieces

Nutty Passion Fruit Yogurts

■ Halve the passion fruit and scoop the pulp into a large bowl. Add the yogurt and mix them together gently.

■ Put 2 tablespoons of the honey in the bases of two narrow glasses and scatter with half of the hazelnuts. Spoon half of the yogurt over the nuts and arrange half of the clementine pieces on top of the yogurt.

■ Repeat the layering, reserving a few of the nuts for decoration. Scatter the nuts over the top and chill the yogurts until you are ready to serve them.

MAKES 12

Calories per serving 120
Preparation time 20 minutes
Cooking time about 10 minutes

INGREDIENTS

1 50 g (2 oz) butter, diced

2 50 g (2 oz) sultanas

3 grated rind of 1 orange

4 1 egg

5 about 125 ml (4 fl oz) milk

STORECUPBOARD

125 g (4oz) self-raising flour, plus extra for
dusting; 100 g (3½ oz) wholemeal self-raising
flour; 2 teaspoons baking powder; 1 tablespoon
caster sugar

Orange & Sultana Scones

■ Sift the flours and baking powder into
a large bowl, tipping any bran in the sieve
back into the bowl. Add the butter and
rub in with the fingertips until the mixture
resembles fine breadcrumbs, then stir
in the sultanas, sugar and orange rind.

■ Break the egg into a measuring jug
and beat with a fork. Top up with milk
up to 150 ml (¼ pint), pour into the flour
mixture and form a soft dough, adding
a little extra milk if the dough is too dry.

■ Press gently into a round, 1 cm (½ inch)
thick, and stamp out about 12 scones. Place
them on lightly floured baking sheets and
brush with a little milk. Bake in a preheated
oven, 220°C (425°F), Gas Mark 7, for
about 10 minutes or until risen and golden.
Allow the scones to cool on a wire rack.
The scones can be stored in an airtight
container for up to 3 days.

MAKES 12

Calories per muffin 214
Preparation time 15 minutes
Cooking time 25 minutes

INGREDIENTS

1	1 egg, beaten

2	200 ml (7 fl oz) milk

3	200 g (7 oz) mixed berries, roughly chopped

STORECUPBOARD

250 g (8 oz) plain flour; 4 tablespoons caster sugar; 1 tablespoon baking powder; 50 ml (2 fl oz) vegetable oil

Very Berry Muffins

■ Mix together all of the ingredients, except the berries, to make a smooth dough. Fold in the berries.

■ Put nonstick paper cases in a 12-section muffin tin and spoon the mixture into the cases. Bake in a preheated oven, 180°C (350°F), Gas Mark 4, for 25 minutes or until a skewer comes out clean when inserted. Transfer to a wire rack to cool.

SERVES 2

Calories per serving 265
Preparation time 5 minutes

INGREDIENTS

1 1 orange, segmented

2 1 banana

3 150 ml (¼ pint) skimmed milk

4 150 g (5 oz) natural yogurt

5 25 g (1 oz) walnut pieces

Walnut & Banana Sunrise Smoothie

■ Place all the ingredients in a food processor or blender and process until the mixture is smooth and frothy. Pour into 2 glasses and serve.

SERVES 4

Calories per serving 171
Preparation time 5 minutes
Cooking time 5 minutes

INGREDIENTS

1 8 large blinis

2 2 tablespoons light crème fraîche

3 1 teaspoon chopped dill

4 2 spring onions, sliced

5 100 g (3½ oz) smoked salmon

STORECUPBOARD

grated rind of 1 lemon; lemon wedges, to garnish;
black pepper

Smoked Salmon Blinis with Dill Cream

■ Gently warm the blinis for a few minutes
under a grill or in the oven.

■ Stir together the crème fraîche, dill,
lemon rind and spring onions and season
with pepper. Spoon the mixture on to the
blinis and top with the salmon. Garnish
with lemon wedges and serve.

SERVES 4

Calories per serving 99
Preparation time 10 minutes, plus cooling
Cooking time 10 minutes

INGREDIENTS

1   2 aubergines, cut into small cubes

2   2 tablespoons capers, roughly chopped

3   4 tomatoes, chopped

4   4 tablespoons chopped parsley

STORECUPBOARD

2 tablespoons olive oil; 1 red onion, finely sliced; 1 tablespoon balsamic vinegar

Warm Aubergine Salad

■ Heat the oil in a nonstick frying pan. Add the aubergines and fry for 10 minutes until golden and softened. Add the red onion, capers, tomatoes, parsley and vinegar and stir to combine.

■ Remove the pan from the heat and leave to cool for 10 minutes before serving.

SERVES 4

Calories per serving 278
Preparation time 20 minutes
Cooking time 30 minutes

INGREDIENTS

1	**4 shallots, thinly sliced**
2	**8 eggs, lightly beaten**
3	**2 tablespoons finely chopped fresh mixed herbs, such as chives, chervil, parsley, basil and thyme**
4	**200 g (7 oz) yellow and red cherry tomatoes, halved**
5	**150 g (5 oz) wafer-thin smoked ham slices**

STORECUPBOARD

4 teaspoons extra virgin rapeseed oil; salt and black pepper

Ham & Tomato Omelettes

■ Heat 1 teaspoon of the oil in a medium-sized frying pan over a medium-low heat, add the shallots and cook gently for 4–5 minutes or until softened.

■ Meanwhile, beat together the eggs and herbs in a large jug and season with salt and pepper.

■ Remove three-quarters of the shallots from the pan with a slotted spoon and set aside. Pour one-quarter of the egg mixture into the pan, then scatter over one-quarter of the cherry tomatoes and stir gently, using a heat-resistant rubber spatula, until the egg is almost set. Scatter one-quarter of the sliced ham evenly over the top of the omelette and cook gently for a further 1 minute.

■ Fold the omelette in half, slide out of the pan on to a warm plate and serve immediately. Repeat with the remaining ingredients to make 3 more omelettes. Alternatively, keep the cooked omelettes warm until all 4 are ready and serve at the same time.

SERVES 4

Calories per serving 262
Preparation time 10 minutes
Cooking time 5 minutes

INGREDIENTS

1 4 spring onions, sliced

2 2 × 400 g (13 oz) cans green lentils, drained and rinsed

3 3 tablespoons chopped herbs (such as parsley, oregano or basil)

4 125 g (4 oz) cherry tomatoes, halved

5 85 g (3¼ oz) sliced Parma ham

STORECUPBOARD

2 tablespoons olive oil; 1 garlic clove, crushed; 2 tablespoons balsamic vinegar

Herby Lentil Salad with Parma Ham Crisps

■ Heat the oil in a nonstick saucepan, add the garlic and spring onions and fry together for 2 minutes.

■ Stir in the lentils, vinegar, herbs and tomatoes and set aside.

■ Heat a frying pan until hot, add the Parma ham and cook for 1–2 minutes, until crisp. Arrange the lentil salad on a large serving dish, place the ham on top and serve immediately.

SERVES 4

Calories per serving 293
Preparation time 15 minutes
Cooking time 5–6 minutes

INGREDIENTS

1	**250 g (8 oz) mini chicken breast fillets**
2	**8 slices granary bread**
3	**6 tablespoons low-fat natural yogurt**
4	**½–1 teaspoon freshly grated hot horseradish or horseradish sauce, to taste**
5	**100 g (3½ oz) mixed salad leaves with beetroot strips**

STORECUPBOARD

8 teaspoons balsamic vinegar; black pepper

Seared Chicken Sandwich

■ Put the mini chicken breast fillets into a plastic bag with half the vinegar and toss together until evenly coated.

■ Heat a nonstick frying pan, lift the chicken out of the bag with a fork and add the pieces to the pan. Fry for 3 minutes, turn and drizzle with the vinegar from the bag and cook for 2–3 more minutes or until browned and cooked through.

■ Toast the bread lightly. Slice the chicken into long, thin strips and arrange them on 4 slices of toast. Mix together the yogurt and horseradish and a little pepper to taste. Add the salad leaves and toss together.

■ Spoon the yogurt and salad leaves over the chicken, drizzle over the remaining vinegar, if liked, and top with the remaining slices of toast. Cut each sandwich in half and serve immediately.

ADD A GARLIC KICK

Toss the chicken fillets with the juice of ½ lemon and 1 tablespoon olive oil then fry as for the main recipe but without the vinegar. Toast 8 slices wholemeal bread then spread with 4 tablespoons garlic mayonnaise. Divide the chicken between 4 slices of toast then top with the shredded leaves of 2 Little Gem lettuces and a 5 cm (2 inch) piece cucumber, thinly sliced. Cover with the remaining slices of toast then press together and cut into triangles. Calories per serving 380

Calories per serving 200
Preparation time 10 minutes, plus standing

INGREDIENTS

1 2 × 400 g (13 oz) cans chickpeas, drained and rinsed

2 4 tomatoes, chopped

3 handful of herbs (such as mint and parsley), chopped

4 pinch of paprika

5 pinch of ground cumin

STORECUPBOARD

1 red onion, finely sliced; 4 tablespoons lemon juice; 1 tablespoon olive oil; salt and black pepper

Moroccan Chickpea Salad

■ Mix together all the ingredients in a large non-metallic bowl. Set aside for 10 minutes to allow the flavours to infuse, then serve.

SERVES 4

Calories per serving 257
Preparation time 10 minutes
Cooking time 3 minutes

INGREDIENTS

| 1 | 250 g (8 oz) wild strawberries, hulled |

| 2 | 12 king scallops, without corals, cut into 3 slices |

| 3 | 3 leeks, cut into matchstick-thin strips |

| 4 | 250 g (8 oz) mixed salad leaves |

| 5 | 12 wild strawberries or 5 larger strawberries, chopped, plus 8 wild strawberries or 3 larger strawberries halved, to garnish |

STORECUPBOARD

2 tablespoons balsamic vinegar; 1 tablespoon lemon juice, plus juice of 1 lemon; 65 ml (2½ fl oz) olive oil; salt and black pepper

Warm Scallop Salad

■ Put the strawberries, vinegar, 1 tablespoon lemon juice and 50 ml (2 fl oz) of the oil in a food processor or blender and process until smooth. Pass through a fine sieve or muslin cloth to remove pips and set aside.

■ Season the scallops with salt and pepper and the remaining lemon juice.

■ Prepare the garnish. Heat the remaining oil in a nonstick frying pan, add the leeks and cook over a high heat, stirring, for 1 minute, or until golden brown. Remove and set aside.

■ Add the scallop slices to the pan and cook for 20–30 seconds each side. Divide the salad leaves across 4 serving plates. Arrange the scallop slices over the salad.

■ Heat the strawberry mixture gently in a small saucepan for 20–30 seconds, then pour over the scallops and salad leaves. Scatter over the leeks and garnish with the halved strawberries. Sprinkle with a little pepper and serve.

ADD A DRESSING

Whisk together 2 tablespoons extra virgin olive oil, 1 teaspoon sesame oil, 1 tablespoon light soy sauce, 2 teaspoons balsamic vinegar, 1 teaspoon clear honey and pepper to taste in a bowl. Cook the scallops as for the main recipe (omitting the leeks) and arrange over the salad. Heat the dressing gently as for the main recipe, then pour over the scallops and salad leaves. Calories per serving 173

SERVES 4

Calories per serving 250
Preparation time 10 minutes, plus cooling
Cooking time 10 minutes

INGREDIENTS

1 3 red peppers, halved, cored and deseeded

2 1 red chilli, deseeded and sliced

3 75 g (3 oz) kabanos sausage, thinly sliced

4 2 × 410 g (13½ oz) cans butter or flageolet beans, rinsed and drained

5 2 tablespoons chopped fresh coriander

STORECUPBOARD

1 tablespoon olive oil; 1 onion, sliced; 1 tablespoon balsamic vinegar

Bean, Kabanos & Pepper Salad

■ Put the peppers on a baking sheet, skin side up, and cook under a preheated hot grill for 8-10 minutes until the skins are blackened. Cover with damp kitchen paper. When the peppers are cool enough to handle, remove the skins and slice the flesh.

■ Meanwhile heat the oil in a nonstick frying pan, add the onion and fry for 5-6 minutes until soft. Add the kabanos sausage and fry for 1-2 minutes until crisp.

■ Mix together the beans and balsamic vinegar, then add the onion and kabanos mixture and the peppers and chilli.

A VEGETARIAN VERSION

Omit the kabanos sausage and mix 50 g (2 oz) halved pitted black olives with the beans. Slice and grill 75 g (3 oz) haloumi. Divide the salad among bowls and top with the haloumi. Calories per serving 248

SERVES 4

Calories per serving 99
Preparation time 10 minutes
Cooking time 2 minutes

INGREDIENTS

1	1 tablespoon black sesame seeds
2	500 g (1 lb) watermelon, peeled, deseeded and diced
3	175 g (6 oz) feta cheese, diced
4	2½ handfuls of rocket
5	handful of mint

STORECUPBOARD

2 tablespoons olive oil; juice of ½ large lemon; salt and black pepper

Watermelon & Feta Salad

■ Dry-fry the sesame seeds for a few minutes until aromatic, then set aside. Arrange the watermelon and feta on a large serving plate with the rocket and mint.

■ Whisk together the olive oil and lemon juice, then season to taste with salt and pepper. Drizzle over the salad, scatter over the sesame seeds and serve.

Calories per serving 186
Preparation time 20 minutes
Cooking time 25 minutes

INGREDIENTS

1   375 g (12 oz), or 3 small, different coloured peppers

2   500 g (1 lb) tomatoes, skinned, deseeded and chopped

3   6 large eggs

4   thyme sprigs, leaves removed, or large pinch of dried thyme, plus extra sprigs to garnish

5   125 g (4 oz) pastrami, thinly sliced

STORECUPBOARD

2 tablespoons olive oil; salt and black pepper; 1 onion, finely chopped; 2 garlic cloves, crushed

Piperade with Pastrami

■ Make the sofrito. Put the peppers on a baking sheet, skin side up, and cook under a preheated hot grill for 8–10 minutes until the skins are blackened. Cover with damp kitchen paper. When the peppers are cool enough to handle, remove the skins, deseed and cut the flesh into strips.

■ Heat 1 tablespoon of the the oil in a large frying pan, add the onion and cook gently for 10 minutes until softened and transparent. Add the garlic, tomatoes and peppers and simmer for 5 minutes until all the juices have evaporated from the tomatoes. Set aside until ready to serve.

■ Beat the eggs together with the thyme and salt and pepper in a bowl. Reheat the sofrito. Heat the remaining oil in a saucepan, add the eggs, stirring until they are lightly scrambled. Stir into the reheated sofrito and spoon on to plates.

■ Arrange slices of pastrami around the eggs and serve immediately, garnished with a little extra thyme.

SERVES 4

Calories per serving 190
Preparation time 15 minutes, plus marinating
Cooking time 3 minutes

INGREDIENTS

1	**400 g (13 oz) can borlotti beans, drained and rinsed**
2	**1 red chilli, deseeded and finely chopped**
3	**2 celery sticks, thinly sliced**
4	**200 g (7 oz) can tuna in olive oil, drained and flaked**
5	**50 g (2 oz) wild rocket leaves**

STORECUPBOARD

1 tablespoon water (optional); 2 tablespoons extra virgin olive oil; 2 garlic cloves, crushed; ½ red onion, cut into thin wedges; finely grated rind and juice of 1 lemon; salt and black pepper

Tuna & Borlotti Bean Salad

■ Heat the borlotti beans in a saucepan over a medium heat for 3 minutes, adding the measurement water if starting to stick to the base.

■ Put the oil, garlic and chilli in a large bowl. Stir in the celery, onion and hot beans and season with salt and pepper. Cover and leave to marinate at room temperature for at least 30 minutes and up to 4 hours.

■ Stir in the tuna and lemon rind and juice. Gently toss in the rocket leaves, taste and adjust the seasoning with extra salt, pepper and lemon juice, if necessary.

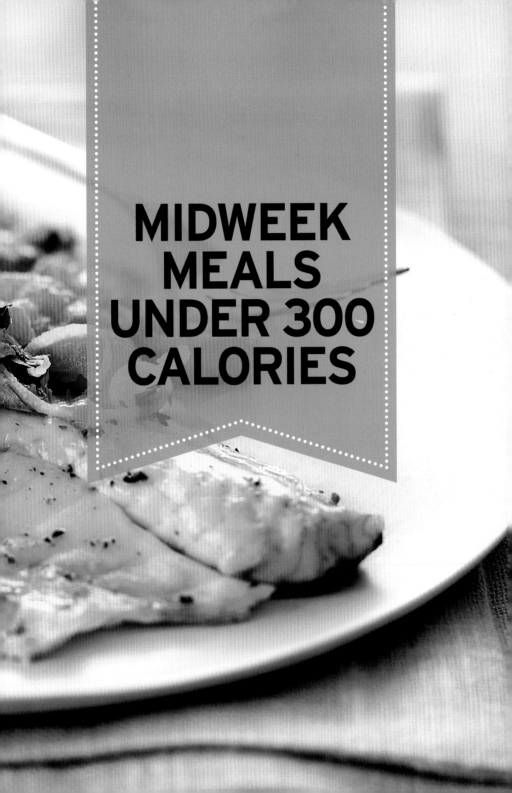

MIDWEEK MEALS UNDER 300 CALORIES

SERVES 4

Calories per serving 239
Preparation time 5 minutes
Cooking time 15 minutes

INGREDIENTS

1	250 g (8 oz) cherry tomatoes, halved
2	100 g (3½ oz) pitted black olives
3	2 tablespoons capers in brine, drained
4	2 tablespoons finely chopped fresh mixed herbs, including thyme and parsley
5	4 cod fillets, about 175 g (6 oz) each

STORECUPBOARD

2 tablespoons extra virgin olive oil; 2 tablespoons balsamic vinegar; salt and black pepper

Baked Cod with Tomatoes & Olives

■ Combine the tomatoes, olives, capers and herbs in a roasting tin. Nestle the cod fillets in the pan, drizzle over the oil and balsamic vinegar and season to taste with salt and pepper.

■ Bake in a preheated oven, 200°C (400°F), Gas Mark 6, for 15 minutes.

■ Transfer the fish, tomatoes and olives to warmed plates. Spoon the pan juices over the fish. Serve immediately.

SERVES 4

Calories per serving 197
Preparation time 10 minutes
Cooking time 16–20 minutes

INGREDIENTS

1	**8 boneless chicken thighs**
2	**2 tablespoons Dijon mustard**
3	**6 drops Tabasco sauce**
4	**1 tablespoon soy sauce**
5	**salad leaves, to serve**

STORECUPBOARD

2 garlic cloves, crushed

Devilled Chicken

■ Heat a large griddle pan (or ordinary frying pan).

■ Remove the skin from the chicken thighs, open them out and trim away any excess fat.

■ To make the devil sauce, mix together the mustard, Tabasco, garlic and soy sauce in a shallow dish.

■ Dip the trimmed chicken thighs in the devil sauce and coat each piece well. Place the chicken pieces flat on the pan and cook in 2 batches for 8–10 minutes on each side.

■ Serve hot or cold with salad leaves.

HOT CHICKEN

Mix 3 tablespoons jerk marinade (a ready-made paste) with the grated rind and juice of ½ an orange and 2 finely chopped cloves of garlic. Dip the chicken in this mixture then cook as for the main recipe. Serve with rice or a salad. Calories per serving 193

SERVES 4

Calories per serving 268
Preparation time 10 minutes
Cooking time 20–25 minutes

INGREDIENTS

| 1 | 2 tablespoons medium curry paste |

| 2 | 1.5 kg (3 lb) prepared mixed vegetables (such as courgette, pepper, mushrooms, green beans and potato – no more than 0.5 kg/1 lb potato) |

| 3 | 200 g (7 oz) can chopped tomatoes |

| 4 | 400 g (13 oz) can reduced-fat coconut milk |

| 5 | 2 tablespoons chopped coriander leaves |

STORECUPBOARD

1 tablespoon olive oil; 1 onion, chopped; 1 garlic clove, crushed

Vegetable Curry

■ Heat the oil in a large saucepan, add the onion and garlic and fry for 2 minutes. Stir in the curry paste and continue frying for 1 minute more.

■ Add the vegetables and fry for 2–3 minutes, stirring occasionally, then add the canned tomatoes and coconut milk. Stir well, bring to the boil, then lower the heat and simmer for 12–15 minutes until all the vegetables are cooked.

■ Stir in the coriander and serve.

SERVES 4

Calories per serving 230
Preparation time 20 minutes
Cooking time 25–30 minutes

INGREDIENTS

1   **400 g (13 oz) raw beetroot, peeled and diced**

2   **625 g (1¼ lb) pumpkin or butternut squash, peeled, deseeded and cut into slightly larger dice**

3   **2 teaspoons fennel seeds**

4   **2 small goats' cheeses, 100 g (3½ oz) each**

5   **chopped rosemary, to garnish**

STORECUPBOARD

1 red onion, cut into wedges; 2 tablespoons olive oil; salt and black pepper

Pumpkin & Goats' Cheese Bake

■ Put the beetroot, pumpkin and onion into a roasting tin, drizzle with the oil and sprinkle with the fennel seeds and salt and pepper. Roast the vegetables in a preheated oven, 200°C (400°F), Gas Mark 6, for 20–25 minutes, turning once, until well browned and tender.

■ Cut the goats' cheeses in half and nestle each half among the roasted vegetables. Sprinkle them with a little salt and pepper and drizzle with some of the pan juices.

■ Return the dish to the oven for about 5 minutes more, until the cheese is just beginning to melt. Sprinkle with rosemary and serve immediately.

SERVES 4

Calories per serving 237
Preparation time 10 minutes
Cooking time 30 minutes

INGREDIENTS

| 1 | 8 plum tomatoes, halved |

| 2 | 4 sea bass fillets, about 150 g (5 oz) each |

| 3 | 2 tablespoons chopped basil, plus leaves to garnish |

STORECUPBOARD

2 tablespoons juice and grated rind of 1 lemon, plus wedges to garnish; 2 tablespoons extra virgin olive oil; salt and black pepper

Bass with Tomato & Basil Sauce

■ Make the sauce up to 2 days in advance. Arrange the tomatoes in a roasting tin, season well and cook in a preheated oven, 200°C (400°F), Gas Mark 6, for 20 minutes.

■ Transfer the tomatoes and any cooking juices to a pan and heat through gently with the lemon juice and most of the rind. Season to taste and set aside until ready to serve.

■ Season the fish fillets and cook under a preheated hot grill for approximately 10 minutes or until the fish is cooked through.

■ Meanwhile, warm the sauce through. Stir the chopped basil and oil through the sauce and spoon it over the fish. Garnish with basil leaves, the rest of the lemon rind and lemon wedges.

SWITCH TO PRAWNS

Replace the bass fillets with 16 raw, peeled tiger prawns. Fry the prawns in a little oil spray until pink and cooked through. Make the sauce as for the main recipe and spoon over the top of the cooked prawns to serve. Calories per serving 169

Calories per serving 282
Preparation time 10 minutes
Cooking time 20–25 minutes

INGREDIENTS

1	2 tablespoons butter or margarine
2	200 g (7 oz) wild mushrooms, trimmed and sliced
3	8 large eggs, beaten
4	2 tablespoons chopped parsley
5	50 g (2 oz) Gruyère cheese, grated

STORECUPBOARD

black pepper

Wild Mushroom Omelette

■ Melt a little of the butter or margarine in an omelette pan, add the mushrooms and sauté for 5–6 minutes until cooked and any moisture has evaporated. Remove the mushrooms from the pan.

■ Melt a little more butter or margarine in the same pan and add one-quarter of the beaten egg. Season well with pepper and stir with a wooden spoon, bringing the cooked egg to the centre of the pan and allowing the runny egg to flow to the edge of the pan and cook.

■ When there is only a little liquid egg left, sprinkle over a quarter of the mushrooms and some of the parsley and Gruyère. Fold the omelette over, tip on to a warm serving plate and keep warm while you make 3 more omelettes in the same way.

SERVES 6

Calories per serving 248
Preparation time 10 minutes
Cooking time 25–30 minutes

INGREDIENTS

| 1 | 450 g (14½ oz) peeled butternut squash, diced |

| 2 | 8 eggs |

| 3 | 1 tablespoon chopped thyme |

| 4 | 2 tablespoons chopped sage |

| 5 | 125 g (4 oz) ricotta cheese |

STORECUPBOARD

1 tablespoon extra virgin rapeseed oil; 1 red onion, thinly sliced; salt and black pepper

Butternut Squash & Ricotta Frittata

■ Heat the oil in a large, deep frying pan with an ovenproof handle over a medium-low heat, add the onion and butternut squash, then cover loosely and cook gently, stirring frequently, for 18–20 minutes or until softened and golden.

■ Lightly beat the eggs, thyme, sage and ricotta in a jug, season the mixture well with salt and pepper and pour over the butternut squash.

■ Cook for a further 2–3 minutes until the egg is almost set, stirring occasionally with a heat-resistant rubber spatula to prevent the base from burning.

■ Slide the pan under a preheated grill, keeping the handle away from the heat, and grill for 3–4 minutes or until the egg is set and the frittata is golden. Slice into 6 wedges and serve hot.

SERVES 4

Calories per serving 136
Preparation time 5 minutes
Cooking time 15 minutes

INGREDIENTS

1 2 smoked bacon rashers, chopped

2 a few sprigs of thyme or lemon thyme

3 2 × 400 g (13 oz) cans cannellini beans, drained and rinsed

4 2 tablespoons chopped parsley

STORECUPBOARD

1 teaspoon olive oil; 2 garlic cloves, crushed; 1 onion, chopped; 900 ml (1½ pints) vegetable stock; black pepper

Bacon & White Bean Soup

■ Heat the oil in a large saucepan, then add the bacon, garlic and onion and fry for 3–4 minutes until the bacon is beginning to brown and the onion to soften.

■ Add the thyme and continue to fry for 1 minute. Then add the beans and stock to the pan, bring to the boil and simmer for 10 minutes.

■ Transfer the soup to a liquidizer or food processor and blend with the parsley and pepper until smooth.

■ Return to the pan and heat through to serve.

SERVES 4

Calories per serving 149
Preparation time 10 minutes
Cooking time 15 minutes

INGREDIENTS

1	4 chicken thighs, skinned and boned
2	2 tablespoons clear honey
3	2 tablespoons mild wholegrain mustard
4	1 courgette, cut into 8 large pieces
5	1 carrot, cut into 8 large pieces

Chicken & Vegetable Skewers

■ Cut the chicken thighs into bite-sized pieces and toss in the honey and mustard. Arrange the chicken pieces on a baking sheet and bake in a preheated oven, 180°C (350°F), Gas Mark 4, for 15 minutes until cooked through and lightly golden. Set aside and leave to cool.

■ Take 8 bamboo skewers and thread with the cooked chicken pieces and the raw vegetables.

■ Serve with the honey and mustard mixture for dipping. The skewers can also be refrigerated for adding to the following day's lunchbox.

ADD A STICKY GLAZE

Mix together 2 tablespoons tomato ketchup, 2 teaspoons runny honey, 2 finely chopped cloves of garlic and 1 tablespoon of sunflower oil. Dip the chicken into the ketchup mixture then cook as for the main recipe. Thread on to skewers with 1 red pepper, deseeded, cored and cut into chunks and 8 cherry tomatoes. Calories per serving 158

SERVES 4

Calories per serving 187 (excluding potatoes
or pasta)
Preparation time 5 minutes
Cooking time 10 minutes

INGREDIENTS

| 1 | 15 g (½ oz) unsalted butter |

| 2 | 50 g (2 oz) pancetta or smoked bacon, finely chopped |

| 3 | 500 g (1 lb) raw, peeled tiger prawns |

| 4 | 1 large bunch of watercress |

STORECUPBOARD

1 teaspoon olive oil; grated rind and juice of
1 lemon

Tiger Prawns with Pancetta

■ Heat the oil and butter in a large frying
pan, add the pancetta or smoked bacon
and fry for 3–4 minutes until crisp.

■ Add the prawns and fry for 1 minute on
each side. Sprinkle over the lemon rind and
juice and continue to fry for 1 minute, then
add the watercress and combine well.

■ Serve as a small lunch or with potatoes
or pasta as a larger main course.

Calories per serving 216
Preparation time 10 minutes
Cooking time 5 minutes

INGREDIENTS

1 1½ tablespoons ready-made or homemade Thai red curry paste

2 375 g (12 oz) lean pork, sliced into thin strips

3 100 g (7 oz) French beans, topped and cut in half

4 2 tablespoons Thai fish sauce (nampla)

5 Chinese chives or regular chives, to garnish

STORECUPBOARD

2 tablespoons groundnut oil; 1 teaspoon caster sugar

Thai Red Pork & Bean Curry

■ Heat the oil in a wok over a medium heat until the oil starts to shimmer. Add the curry paste and cook, stirring, until it releases its aroma.

■ Add the pork and French beans and stir-fry for 2–3 minutes until the meat is cooked through and the beans are just tender.

■ Stir in the fish sauce and sugar and serve, garnished with chives.

SERVES 6

Calories per serving 218
Preparation time 10 minutes
Cooking time 15–20 minutes

INGREDIENTS

1	125 g (4 oz) orzo, macaroni or other small pasta shapes
2	25 g (1 oz) butter
3	4 egg yolks
4	125 g (4 oz) cooked chicken, torn into fine shreds
5	oregano leaves

STORECUPBOARD

2 litres (3½ pints) chicken stock; 25 g (1 oz) plain flour; grated rind and juice of 1 lemon, plus extra lemon rind and lemon wedges; salt and black pepper

Greek Chicken Avgolomeno

■ Bring the stock to the boil, add the pasta and simmer for 8–10 minutes until just tender.

■ Meanwhile, heat the butter in a separate smaller pan, stir in the flour then gradually mix in 2 ladlefuls of the stock from the large pan. Bring to the boil, stirring. Take off the heat.

■ Mix the egg yolks in a medium-sized bowl with the lemon rind and some salt and pepper. Gradually mix in the lemon juice until smooth. Slowly mix in the hot sauce from the small pan, stirring continuously.

■ Stir a couple more hot ladlefuls of stock into the lemon mixture once the pasta is cooked, then pour this into the large pasta pan. (Don't be tempted to add the eggs and lemon straight into the pasta pan or it may curdle.) Mix well, then ladle into shallow soup bowls and top with the chicken, some extra lemon rind and some torn oregano leaves. Serve with lemon wedges.

SERVES 4

Calories per serving 160
Preparation time 15 minutes
Cooking time 25 minutes

INGREDIENTS

| **1** | 4 lean back bacon rashers, chopped |

| **2** | 500 g (1 lb) sweet potatoes, chopped |

| **3** | 2 parsnips, chopped |

| **4** | 1 teaspoon chopped thyme |

| **5** | 1 baby Savoy cabbage, shredded |

STORECUPBOARD

2 onions, chopped; 2 garlic cloves, sliced; 900 ml (1½ pints) vegetable stock

Sweet Potato & Cabbage Soup

■ Place the onions, garlic and bacon in a large saucepan and fry for 2–3 minutes.

■ Add the sweet potatoes, parsnips, thyme and stock, bring to the boil and simmer for 15 minutes.

■ Transfer two-thirds of the soup to a liquidizer or food processor and blend until smooth. Return to the pan, add the cabbage and continue to simmer for 5–7 minutes until the cabbage is just cooked.

TRY IT WITH BROCCOLI

Follow the main recipe, replacing the sweet potatoes with 500 g (1 lb) peeled and chopped butternut squash. After returning the blended soup to the pan, add 100 g (3½ oz) broccoli, broken into small florets. Cook as for the main recipe, omitting the cabbage. Calories per serving 160

SERVES 6

Calories per serving 122
Preparation time 5 minutes
Cooking time 10 minutes

INGREDIENTS

1	1 kg (2 lb) large, uncooked langoustine prawns in their shells (thawed if frozen)
2	4 cm (1½ inch) piece of fresh root ginger, peeled and finely chopped
3	2 teaspoons tamarind paste
4	juice of 2 limes and lime wedges
5	small bunch of coriander, torn into pieces

STORECUPBOARD

2 tablespoons olive oil; 1 large onion, chopped;
3-4 garlic cloves, finely chopped; 300 ml (½ pint)
fish stock

Prawns with Tamarind & Lime

■ Rinse the prawns in cold water and drain well. Heat the oil in a large saucepan or wok, add the onion and fry for 5 minutes until just beginning to brown.

■ Stir in the garlic, ginger and tamarind paste, then mix in the lime juice and stock.

■ Bring the stock to the boil, add the prawns and cook, stirring, for 5 minutes until the prawns are bright pink. Spoon into bowls and serve garnished with the torn coriander leaves and lime wedges.

Calories per serving 107
Preparation time 15 minutes
Cooking time 25 minutes

INGREDIENTS

| 1 | 150 ml (¼ pint) marsala or sweet sherry |

| 2 | 1 vanilla pod |

| 3 | 6 peaches, halved and pitted |

| 4 | 150 g (5 oz) fresh raspberries |

STORECUPBOARD

250 ml (8 fl oz) water; 75 g (3 oz) caster sugar

Poached Peaches & Raspberries

■ Pour the water and marsala or sherry into a saucepan and add the sugar. Slit the vanilla pod lengthways and scrape out the black seeds from inside the pod. Add these to the water with the pod, then gently heat the mixture until the sugar has dissolved.

■ Place the peach halves, cut side down, in an overproof dish so that they sit together snugly. Pour over the hot syrup, then cover and cook in a preheated oven, 180°F (350°F), Gas Mark 4, for 20 minutes.

■ Scatter over the raspberries. Serve the fruit either warm or cold. Spoon into serving bowls and decorate with the vanilla pod cut into thin strips.

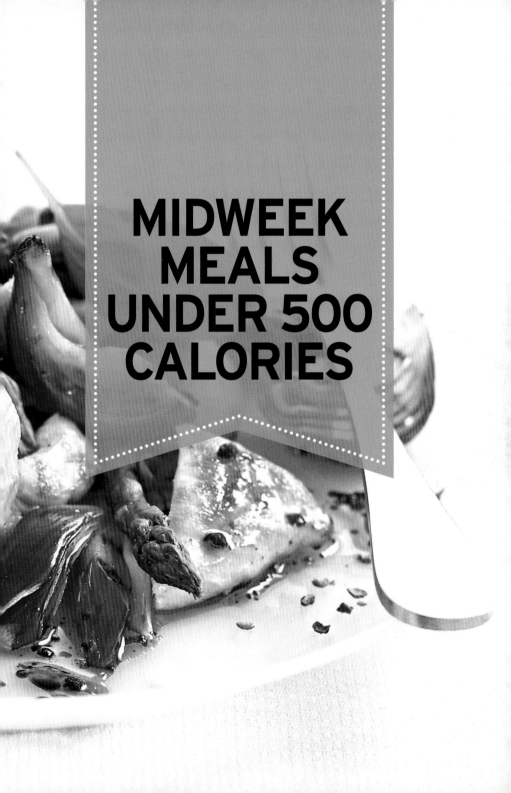

MIDWEEK MEALS UNDER 500 CALORIES

SERVES 4

Calories per serving 498
Preparation time 10 minutes
Cooking time 10 minutes

INGREDIENTS

1	4 mini pizza bases
2	250 g (8 oz) reduced-fat mozzarella cheese, shredded
3	8 cherry tomatoes, quartered
4	150 g (5 oz) prosciutto, sliced
5	50 g (2 oz) rocket leaves, washed

STORECUPBOARD

2 garlic cloves, halved; balsamic vinegar, to taste; salt and black pepper

Quick Prosciutto & Rocket Pizza

■ Rub the top surfaces of the pizza bases with the cut faces of the garlic cloves and discard the cloves.

■ Put the pizza bases on a baking sheet, top with mozzarella and tomatoes and bake in a preheated oven, 200°C (400°F), Gas Mark 6, for 10 minutes until the bread is golden.

■ Top the pizzas with prosciutto and rocket leaves, season to taste with salt, pepper and balsamic vinegar and serve immediately.

MAKE A HAWAIIAN

Drain and chop a 220 g (7½ oz) can pineapple rings, and drain and flake a 160 g (5½ oz) can tuna in spring water. Top the pizza bases with the pineapple and tuna then scatter over the mozzarella and tomatoes before cooking as for the main recipe. Calories per serving 481

SERVES 4

Calories per serving 340
Preparation time 5 minutes, plus marinating
Cooking time 5–6 minutes

INGREDIENTS

1   4 boneless, skinless chicken breasts, about 500 g (1 lb) in total, cut into 2.5 cm (1 inch) cubes

2   4 tablespoons dark soy sauce, plus extra to serve

3   4 tablespoons mirin

4   250 g (8 oz) soba noodles

STORECUPBOARD

2 tablespoons caster sugar; sesame oil, to serve

Chicken Teriyaki

■ Place the chicken in a shallow dish. Combine the soy sauce, mirin and sugar, add to the chicken and toss well to coat. Set aside to marinate for 15 minutes.

■ Meanwhile, cook the noodles according to the packet instructions, then drain, refresh in iced water, drain again and chill.

■ Thread the chicken cubes on to metal skewers and barbecue or grill for 2–3 minutes on each side.

■ Toss the noodles with a little sesame oil and serve with the chicken and extra sesame oil and soy sauce.

SERVES 4

Calories per serving 353
Preparation time 5 minutes
Cooking time 5 minutes

INGREDIENTS

1   **3 sirloin steaks, about 300 g (10 oz) each**

2   **150 g (5 oz) radicchio, sliced into 2.5 cm (1 inch) strips**

STORECUPBOARD

½ tablespoon olive oil; 2 garlic cloves, finely chopped; salt

Beef Strips with Radicchio

■ Trim the fat from the steaks and slice the meat into very thin strips.

■ Heat the oil in a heavy-based frying pan over a high heat, add the garlic and steak strips, season with salt and stir-fry for 2 minutes or until the steak strips are golden brown.

■ Add the radicchio and stir-fry until the leaves are just beginning to wilt. Serve immediately.

SERVES 4

Calories per serving 357
Preparation time 15 minutes
Cooking time 45 minutes

INGREDIENTS

1 | 4 × 125 g (4 oz) boneless, skinless chicken breasts

2 | 2 red peppers, cored, deseeded, cut into flat pieces

3 | 1 bunch asparagus, trimmed

4 | 200 g (7 oz) new potatoes, boiled, cut in half

5 | 1 bunch basil

STORECUPBOARD

2 small red onions; 5 tablespoons olive oil; 2 tablespoons balsamic vinegar; salt and black pepper

Griddled Summer Chicken Salad

■ Heat a griddle pan (or ordinary frying pan). Place the chicken breasts in the pan and cook for 8–10 minutes on each side. When cooked, remove from the pan and cut roughly into chunks.

■ Cut the red onions into wedges, keeping the root ends intact to hold the wedges together. Place in the pan and cook for 5 minutes on each side. Remove from the pan and set aside.

■ Place the flat pieces of red pepper in the pan and cook for 8 minutes on the skin side only, so that the skins are charred and blistered. Remove and set aside, then cook the asparagus in the pan for 6 minutes, turning frequently.

■ Put the boiled potatoes in a large bowl. Tear the basil, keeping a few leaves intact to garnish, and add to the bowl, together with the chicken and all the vegetables. Add the olive oil, balsamic vinegar and seasoning. Toss the salad and garnish with the reserved basil leaves.

SERVES 2

Calories per serving 393
Preparation time 10 minutes
Cooking time 12–16 minutes

INGREDIENTS

1	**350 g (¾ lb) potatoes, peeled and cubed**
2	**3 tablespoons light crème fraîche**
3	**½ tablespoon chopped sage**
4	**2 slices of calves liver, about 150 g (5 oz) each**
5	**gravy, to serve**

STORECUPBOARD

1 garlic clove; 1 tablespoon seasoned flour;
2 tablespoons olive oil; salt and black pepper

Calves' Liver with Garlic Mash

■ Cook the potatoes and garlic in a saucepan of lightly salted boiling water for 10–12 minutes until tender, then drain. Return the potatoes and garlic to the pan and mash with the crème fraîche and sage. Season well with pepper.

■ Meanwhile, press the pieces of liver into the seasoned flour to coat them all over. Heat the oil in a frying pan, add the liver and fry for 1–2 minutes on each side or until cooked to your liking. Serve with the mash and gravy.

SERVES 4

Calories per serving 350
Preparation time 5 minutes
Cooking time 30 minutes

INGREDIENTS

1   **4 red peppers, halved, cored and deseeded, with stalks left on**

2   **400 g (13 oz) can flageolet beans, drained and rinsed**

3   **125 g (4 oz) firm goats' cheese**

4   **8 teaspoons ready-made pesto**

STORECUPBOARD

4 teaspoons olive oil

Grilled Peppers with Goats' Cheese

■ Put the pepper halves on a baking sheet, skin side down, and divide the flageolet beans among them. Drizzle with the oil.

■ Cut the goats' cheese horizontally into 8 slices and arrange the slices on top of the beans. Top each stack with 1 teaspoon pesto.

■ Cover the peppers with foil and bake in a preheated oven, 200°C (400°F), Gas Mark 6, for 20 minutes or until the peppers are tender. Remove the foil and bake for a further 10 minutes.

SERVES 4

Calories per serving 461
Preparation time 10 minutes
Cooking time about 10 minutes

INGREDIENTS

1	200 g (7 oz) chorizo sausage, cut into 1 cm (½ inch) dice
2	2 ripe tomatoes, deseeded and finely chopped
3	3 tablespoons chopped parsley
4	2 × 400 g (13 oz) cans chickpeas, drained

STORECUPBOARD

2 tablespoons olive oil; 1 red onion, finely chopped;
2 garlic cloves, crushed; salt and black pepper

Chickpeas with Chorizo

■ Heat the oil in a large nonstick frying pan, add the onion, garlic and chorizo and cook over a medium-high heat, stirring frequently, for 4–5 minutes.

■ Add the tomatoes, parsley and chickpeas to the pan and cook, stirring frequently, for 4–5 minutes or until the mixture is heated through.

■ Season to taste with salt and pepper and serve immediately or leave to cool to room temperature.

SERVES 4

Calories per serving 451
Preparation time 10 minutes
Cooking time 15 minutes

INGREDIENTS

1	500 g (1 lb) small new potatoes, scrubbed
2	4 fresh tuna steaks, about 175 g (6 oz) each
3	100 g (3½ oz) baby spinach leaves, roughly chopped
4	griddled lime wedges, to serve

STORECUPBOARD

4 tablespoons olive oil; 2 tablespoons balsamic vinegar; salt and black pepper

Griddled Tuna Salad

■ Place the new potatoes in a steamer over boiling water and cook for 15 minutes or until tender.

■ Meanwhile, heat a griddle pan. Pat the tuna fillets dry with kitchen paper and cook in the pan for 3 minutes on each side for rare, 5 minutes for medium or 8 minutes for well done.

■ Remove the potatoes from the steamer. Slice them in half and place in a bowl. Add the spinach, olive oil and balsamic vinegar. Toss and season to taste. Divide the salad between 4 plates and serve with a slice of tuna arranged on the top of each, and a griddled lime wedge for squeezing.

SERVES 4

Calories per serving 413
Preparation time 5 minutes
Cooking time 20–25 minutes

INGREDIENTS

1   4 tablespoons medium curry paste

2   8 boneless, skinless chicken thighs, cut into thin strips

3   400 g (13 oz) can chopped tomatoes

4   250 g (8 oz) broccoli, broken into small florets, stalks peeled and sliced

5   100 ml (3½ fl oz) coconut milk

STORECUPBOARD

3 tablespoons olive oil; 1 onion, finely chopped; salt and black pepper

Fast Chicken Curry

■ Heat the oil in a deep nonstick saucepan over a medium heat. Add the onion and cook for 3 minutes until soft and translucent. Add the curry paste and cook, stirring, for 1 minute until fragrant.

■ Add the chicken, tomatoes, and coconut milk to the pan. Bring to the boil, then reduce the heat, cover and simmer gently over a low heat for 15–20 minutes, adding the broccoli after 10 minutes, until the chicken is cooked through.

■ Remove from the heat, season well with salt and pepper and serve immediately.

SERVES 4

Calories per serving 422
Preparation time 10 minutes
Cooking time 10 minutes

INGREDIENTS

1	4 trout fillets, about 200 g (7 oz) each
2	large handful of basil, roughly chopped, plus extra to garnish
3	50 g (2 oz) Parmesan cheese, freshly grated
4	salad, to serve

STORECUPBOARD

4 tablespoons olive oil, plus extra for greasing; 1 garlic clove, crushed; salt and black pepper

Trout with Pesto

■ Brush a foil-lined baking sheet lightly with oil and place under a preheated very hot grill to heat up.

■ Put the trout fillets on to the hot sheet, sprinkle with salt and pepper and place under the grill for 8–10 minutes until lightly browned and the fish flakes easily when pressed with a knife.

■ Meanwhile, put the basil and garlic into a bowl. Work in the oil using a hand-held blender. Stir in the Parmesan cheese.

■ Remove the fish from the grill, transfer to serving plates, drizzle with the pesto, sprinkle with extra basil leaves to garnish and serve with salad.

A FRUITY VERSION

Put the trout fillets on a foil-lined grill rack as for the main recipe. Mix together the finely grated rind and juice of 1 small orange, 1 tablespoon chopped parsley and 4 tablespoons olive oil. Brush the mixture over the fillets and season with salt and pepper. Grill until golden and opaque, then sprinkle with toasted flaked almonds. Serve with a simple salad. Calories per serving 403

SERVES 4

Calories per serving 401
Preparation time 10 minutes, plus marinating
Cooking time 16–20 minutes

INGREDIENTS

1 4 × 125 g (4 oz) boneless, skinless chicken breasts

2 4 tablespoons tandoori paste or powder

3 4 tomatoes, finely sliced

4 1 bunch fresh coriander, roughly chopped

STORECUPBOARD

2 red onions, finely sliced; 4 tablespoons lemon juice, plus lemon wedges, griddled (optional), to serve; 4 tablespoons olive oil; salt and black pepper

Griddled Tandoori Chicken

■ Using a sharp knife, make a series of small slashes in the flesh of the chicken breasts and rub in the tandoori paste or powder. Leave to marinate in the refrigerator overnight.

■ Heat a griddle pan (or ordinary frying pan). Cook the marinated chicken breasts for 8–10 minutes on each side, allowing the authentic tandoori charred colour to appear, until cooked throroughly.

■ Mix the red onions, tomatoes and coriander together with the lemon juice, olive oil and seasoning in a small bowl. Serve the salad with the tandoori chicken, accompanied by lemon wedges, griddled if liked.

TRY HARISSA

Rub the slashed chicken with
4 teaspoons harissa paste instead
of the tandoori paste or powder.
Marinate then fry. Soak 200 g
(7 oz) couscous in 450 ml (¾ pint)
boiling water for 5 minutes. Stir in
2 tablespoons olive oil, 3 tablespoons
fresh chopped coriander and
seasoning. Serve with lemon
wedges. Calories per serving 402

SERVES 2

Calories per serving 417
Preparation time 10 minutes
Cooking time 15 minutes

INGREDIENTS

| 1 | 400 g (13 oz) can butter beans, drained and rinsed |

| 2 | 200 g (7 oz) baby spinach leaves |

| 3 | 4 eggs, beaten |

| 4 | 50 g (2 oz) ricotta cheese |

STORECUPBOARD

1 teaspoon olive oil; 1 onion, sliced; salt and black pepper (optional)

Spinach & Ricotta Frittata

■ Heat the oil in a medium frying pan, add the onion and fry for 3–4 minutes until softened. Add the butter beans and spinach and heat gently for 2–3 minutes until the spinach has wilted.

■ Pour over the eggs, then spoon over the ricotta and season with salt and pepper if liked. Cook until almost set, then place the pan under a hot grill and cook for another 1–2 minutes until golden and set.

Calories per serving 476
Preparation time 15 minutes
Cooking time 1¾–2¼ hours

INGREDIENTS

1	12 large chicken drumsticks
2	6 tablespoons very finely chopped lemon grass
3	1 lemon grass stalk, halved lengthways
4	1 red chilli, finely sliced or chopped
5	2 tablespoons medium curry paste

STORECUPBOARD

1 tablespoon sunflower oil; 1 onion, finely chopped; 4 garlic cloves, crushed; 1 tablespoon granulated palm sugar; 250 ml (8 fl oz) chicken stock; salt and black pepper

Lemon Grass Chicken

■ Heat the oil in a large, heavy-based casserole dish and brown the drumsticks evenly for 5–6 minutes. Remove with a slotted spoon and set aside.

■ Add the onion and stir-fry over a low heat for 10 minutes. Add the garlic, lemon grass, chilli and curry paste and stir-fry for 1–2 minutes.

■ Return the chicken to the dish with the palm sugar and stock. Bring to the boil, season and cover tightly. Cook in a preheated oven at 140°C (275°F), Gas Mark 1 for 1½–2 hours or until tender. Remove from the oven and serve immediately.

SERVES 4

Calories per serving 435
Preparation time: 10–15 minutes
Cooking time: 35 minutes

INGREDIENTS

1	4 red peppers, cored, deseeded and sliced
2	60 g (2½ oz) walnuts, chopped
3	300 g (10 oz) fresh egg pappardelle
4	25 g (1 oz) Parmesan cheese shavings

STORECUPBOARD

2 teaspoons olive oil; 3–4 large garlic cloves, thinly sliced; salt and black pepper

Pepper & Walnut Pappardelle

■ Put the peppers on a baking sheet, skin side up. Brush with ½ teaspoon of the olive oil and cook under a preheated hot grill until the skins start to blacken. Cover with damp kitchen paper. When the peppers are cool enough to handle, remove the skins.

■ Reserve 4 slices of pepper to use as a garnish and cut the remaining peppers into large dice.

■ Heat the remaining olive oil in a large frying pan over a medium-low heat, add the sliced garlic but do not let it brown. Add the diced red pepper and stir in the walnuts. Keep warm.

■ Bring a large saucepan of lightly salted water to the boil. Add the pasta, return to the boil and cook for 3–4 minutes or until the pasta is al dente. Drain and transfer to a large, warm serving bowl.

■ Toss the pasta well with the garlic, pepper and walnut mixture. Sprinkle over the Parmesan shavings and garnish with the reserved pepper slices.

SERVES 4

Calories per serving 428
Preparation time 10 minutes
Cooking time 25 minutes

INGREDIENTS

1   300 g (10 oz) risotto rice

2   150 ml (¼ pint) dry white wine

3   125 g (4 oz) light cream cheese

4   125 g (4 oz) smoked salmon, chopped

5   4 tablespoons chopped herbs (such as chives, parsley or dill)

STORECUPBOARD

2 teaspoons olive oil; 1 onion, finely chopped; 2 garlic cloves, crushed; 900 ml (1½ pints) simmering vegetable stock; salt and black pepper

Smoked Salmon Risotto

■ Heat the oil in a large saucepan, add the onion and garlic and fry for 2–3 minutes until they begin to soften.

■ Stir in the rice and continue to cook for 1 minute. Add the wine and cook, stirring, until all the wine has been absorbed.

■ Reduce the heat and add the stock a little at a time, stirring continuously, and allowing each amount of stock to be absorbed before adding the next. Continue until all the stock has been absorbed.

■ Stir in the cream cheese, smoked salmon and herbs, season to taste with salt and pepper and serve.

SOMETHING SPECIAL

SERVES 6

Calories per serving 150
Preparation time 10 minutes
Cooking time 6 minutes

INGREDIENTS

1	200 g (7 oz) trimmed asparagus
2	3 tablespoons roughly chopped hazelnuts
3	1 teaspoon Dijon mustard
4	12 quail eggs
5	250 g (8 oz) smoked salmon

STORECUPBOARD

4 teaspoons olive oil; juice of 1 lemon; salt
and black pepper

Asparagus with Smoked Salmon

■ Put the asparagus in a steamer set over a saucepan of boiling water, cover and cook for 5 minutes until just tender.

■ Meanwhile, put the nuts in a foil-lined grill pan and cook under a preheated grill until lightly browned. In a bowl, lightly mix together the oil, lemon juice and mustard with a little salt and pepper, then stir in the hot nuts. Keep warm.

■ Pour water into a saucepan to a depth of 4 cm (1½ inches) and bring it to the boil. Lower the eggs into the water with a slotted spoon and cook for 1 minute. Remove the pan from the heat and leave the eggs to stand for 1 minute. Drain the eggs, then cool under cold running water and drain again.

■ Tear the salmon into strips and divide among 6 serving plates. Do the same with the asparagus, then halve the quail eggs, leaving the shells on if liked, and arrange on top. Drizzle with the warm nut dressing and sprinkle with a little pepper to serve.

SERVES 6

Calories per serving 403
Preparation time 20 minutes
Cooking time 15 minutes

INGREDIENTS

1 3 duck breasts, each about 225 g (7½ oz)

2 300 g (10 oz) green beans, trimmed

3 3 clementines, peeled and segmented; plus juice of 2 clementines

4 200 g (7 oz) spinach or tatsoi

STORECUPBOARD

1 tablespoon white wine vinegar; 4 tablespoons olive oil; salt and black pepper

Duck & Clementine salad

■ Put the duck breasts, skin-side down, in a cold ovenproof dish and cook over a medium heat for 6 minutes or until the skin has turned crisp and brown. Turn them over and cook for a further 2 minutes. Transfer the duck to a preheated oven, 180°C (350°F), Gas Mark 4, and cook for 5 minutes until cooked through. Remove the duck breasts from the oven, cover with foil and leave to rest.

■ Meanwhile, blanch the green beans in lightly salted boiling water for 2 minutes until cooked but still firm and bright green. Drain and refresh in cold water. Transfer the beans to a large salad bowl with the clementine segments.

■ Make the dressing by whisking together the clementine juice, vinegar and oil in a small bowl. Season to taste with salt and pepper if liked.

■ Add the spinach or tatsoi to the beans and clementines, drizzle over the dressing and combine well. Slice the duck meat, combine it with the salad and serve immediately.

SERVES 1

Calories per serving 127
Preparation time 15 minutes, plus marinating
and chilling
Cooking time 15 minutes

INGREDIENTS

1   **125 g (4 oz) cod, coley or haddock fillet**

2   **1 tablespoon fresh coriander leaves**

3   **1 green chilli, deseeded and chopped**

4   **2 teaspoons natural yogurt**

STORECUPBOARD

2 teaspoons lemon juice; 1 garlic clove;
¼ teaspoon sugar

Chilli & Coriander Fish Parcels

■ Place the fish in a non-metallic dish and sprinkle with the lemon juice. Cover and leave in the refrigerator to marinate for 15–20 minutes.

■ Put the coriander, garlic and chilli in a food processor or blender and process until the mixture forms a paste. Add the sugar and yogurt and briefly process to blend.

■ Lay the fish on a sheet of foil. Coat the fish on both sides with the paste. Gather up the foil loosely and turn over at the top to seal. Return to the refrigerator for at least 1 hour.

■ Place the parcel on a baking tray and bake in a preheated oven, 200°C (400°F), Gas Mark 6, for about 15 minutes until the fish is just cooked.

SERVES 4

Calories per serving 424
Preparation time 10 minutes
Cooking time up to 45 minutes

INGREDIENTS

1 750 g (1½ lb) loin of venison, cut from the haunch

2 2 tablespoons juniper berries, crushed

3 1 egg white, lightly beaten

4 400 g (13 oz) green beans

STORECUPBOARD

75 g (3 oz) mixed peppercorns, crushed; salt and black pepper

Pepper-crusted Loin of Venison

■ Make sure that the venison fits into your grill pan; if necessary, cut the loin in half.

■ Combine the peppercorns, juniper berries and some salt in a shallow dish. Dip the venison in the egg white, roll it in the peppercorn mixture, covering it evenly.

■ Cook the venison under a preheated hot grill for 4 minutes on each of the four sides, turning it carefully so that the crust stays intact. Transfer the loin to a lightly greased roasting tin and cook in a preheated oven, 200°C (400°F), Gas Mark 6, for another 15 minutes for rare and up to 30 minutes for well done (the time will depend on the thickness of the loin of venison).

■ Leave the venison to rest for a few minutes, then slice it thickly and serve with green beans and finely sliced sweet potato crisps, if liked.

SERVES 4

Calories per serving 399
Preparation time 10 minutes
Cooking time 10 minutes

INGREDIENTS

1   4 swordfish steaks, about 150 g (5 oz) each

2   4–5 small ripe tomatoes

3   16 Kalamata olives in brine, drained

4   2 tablespoons chopped flat leaf parsley

5   200 g (7 oz) couscous

STORECUPBOARD

salt and black pepper

Swordfish with Couscous & Salsa

■ Season the swordfish steaks with salt and pepper.

■ Dice or quarter the tomatoes and transfer them to a bowl with all the juices. Remove the stones from the olives and chop the flesh if the pieces are still large. Stir them into the tomatoes with the parsley, season to taste and set aside.

■ Cook the couscous according to the instructions on the packet and set aside.

■ Meanwhile, cook the swordfish steaks, 2 at a time, in a preheated hot griddle pan. Cook on the first side for 4 minutes, without disturbing them, then turn and cook for a further minute.

■ Serve the swordfish and couscous immediately with the olive and tomato salsa on the side.

SERVES 4

Calories per serving 293
Preparation time 10 minutes
Cooking time 20 minutes

INGREDIENTS

1   2 × 400 g (13 oz) cans cannellini beans, drained and rinsed

2   2 tablespoons chopped parsley, plus sprigs to garnish

3   16 baby leeks

4   16 large scallops, shelled and prepared

STORECUPBOARD

2 garlic cloves; 200 ml (7 fl oz) vegetable stock; 2 teaspoons olive oil; 3 tablespoons water

Scallops with White Bean Purée

■ Place the beans, garlic and stock in a saucepan, bring to the boil and simmer for 10 minutes. Remove from the heat, drain off any excess liquid, then mash with a potato masher and stir in the parsley. Keep warm.

■ Heat half the oil in a nonstick frying pan, add the leeks and fry for 2 minutes, then add the measurement water. Cover and simmer for 5–6 minutes until tender.

■ Meanwhile, heat the remaining oil in a small frying pan, add the scallops and fry for 1 minute on each side. Serve with the white bean purée and leeks.

Calories per serving 302 (excluding
wholegrain rice)
Preparation time 15 minutes
Cooking time about 30 minutes

INGREDIENTS

1   1 red pepper, halved and deseeded

2   8 dry black olives, pitted

3   2 teaspoons capers

4   8 shallots, peeled

5   4 beef fillet steaks, about 150 g
(5¼ oz) each

STORECUPBOARD

2 garlic cloves; 1 tablespoon olive oil; 50 ml (2 fl oz)
balsamic vinegar; 1 teaspoon light muscovado
sugar; salt and black pepper

Beef Fillet with Red Pepper Crust

■ Cook the pepper under a preheated hot grill until the skin blackens. Remove and cover with damp kitchen paper until it is cool enough to handle, then peel and chop.

■ Blend together the garlic, olives, 1 teaspoon of the oil, the capers and the chopped red pepper.

■ Put the shallots and the remaining oil in a small pan. Cover and cook, stirring frequently, over low heat for 15 minutes. Add the vinegar and sugar and cook uncovered, stirring frequently, for a further 5 minutes.

■ Season the steaks and cook, 2 at a time, in a preheated heavy-based frying pan or griddle pan. Cook on one side, then transfer to a baking sheet. Top each steak with some red pepper mix. Bake in a preheated oven, 200°C (400°F), Gas Mark 6, for 5 minutes or according to taste. Leave to stand in a warm place for 5 minutes before serving with the balsamic shallots and, if liked, steamed wholegrain rice.

TRY IT WITH MUSHROOMS

Blend 350 g (11½ oz) chopped mushrooms with 2 crushed garlic cloves, 1 chopped onion, 1 tablespoon olive oil and seasoning. Cook as for the main recipe for 10 minutes or until reduced down to concentrate. Add juice of ½ lemon, 2 tablespoons chopped fresh parsley and a dash of brandy, then cook for a further 5 minutes. Cook the steaks as for the main recipe and top with the mushroom mixture. Calories per serving 271

SERVES 4

Calories per serving 499
Preparation time 5 minutes
Cooking time 10 minutes

INGREDIENTS

1	**4 salmon fillets, about 200 g (7 oz) each**
2	**1½ teaspoon cumin seeds, crushed**
3	**1 teaspoon smoked or ordinary paprika**
4	**2 courgettes, sliced into thin ribbons**

STORECUPBOARD

3 tablespoons light muscovado sugar; 2 garlic cloves, crushed; 1 tablespoon white wine vinegar; 3 tablespoons groundnut oil; salt and black pepper; lemon wedges, to serve

Sugar & Spice Salmon

■ Put the salmon fillets in a lightly oiled roasting tin. Mix together the sugar, garlic, 1 teaspoon of the cumin seeds, paprika, vinegar and a little salt in a bowl, then spread the mixture all over the fish so that it is thinly coated. Drizzle with 1 tablespoon of the oil.

■ Bake in a preheated oven, 220°C (425°F), Gas Mark 7, for 10 minutes or until the fish is cooked through.

■ Meanwhile, heat the remaining oil in a large frying pan, add the remaining crushed cumin seeds and fry for 10 seconds. Add the courgette ribbons, season with salt and pepper and stir-fry for 2–3 minutes until just softened.

■ Transfer to warm serving plates and serve the salmon on top, garnished with lemon wedges.

SERVES 2

Calories per serving 490
Preparation time 10 minutes
Cooking time 9 minutes

INGREDIENTS

1   1.5 kg (3 lb) small farmed mussels

2   150 ml (¼ pint) dry cider

3   100 g (3½ oz) double cream

4   2 tablespoons chopped parsley

STORECUPBOARD

2 garlic cloves, chopped; 1 onion, diced; salt and black pepper

Mussels with Cider

■ Wash the mussels thoroughly and put in a large saucepan with the garlic, diced onion and cider. Bring to the boil, cover and cook over a medium heat for 4–5 minutes until all the shells have opened. Discard any that remain closed after cooking.

■ Strain the mussels through a colander and put in a large bowl, cover with foil and place in a very low oven to keep warm.

■ Pass the cooking juices through a fine sieve into a clean saucepan and bring to the boil. Whisk in the cream and simmer for 3–4 minutes, or until thickened slightly. Season to taste with salt and pepper.

■ Pour the sauce over the mussels, scatter over the parsley and serve immediately.

ASIAN FLAVOURS

Wash the mussels thoroughly and put in a large saucepan with 2 sliced garlic cloves, 2 teaspoons grated fresh root ginger, 1 finely diced onion and 1 sliced red chilli. Add a splash of water and cook as for the main recipe. Strain the mussels and keep warm. Strain the cooking juices through a fine sieve into a clean saucepan. Whisk in 100 g (3½ oz) coconut cream and heat through. Pour over the mussels and served garnished with chopped fresh coriander. Calories per serving 314

SERVES 4

Calories per serving 411
Preparation time 5 minutes
Cooking time 15–20 minutes

INGREDIENTS

1 4 boneless, skinless chicken breasts, about 200 g (7 oz) each

2 150 ml (¼ pint) freshly squeezed orange juice, plus 1 small orange, sliced

3 2 tablespoons chopped mint

4 1 tablespoon butter

5 200 g (7 oz) couscous

STORECUPBOARD

3 tablespoons olive oil; salt and black pepper

Chicken with Orange & Mint

■ Season the chicken breasts to taste with salt and pepper. Heat the oil in a large nonstick frying pan, add the chicken breasts and cook over a medium heat, turning once, for 4–5 minutes or until golden all over.

■ Pour in the orange juice, add the orange slices, and bring to a gentle simmer. Cover tightly, reduce the heat to low and cook gently for 8–10 minutes or until the chicken is cooked through. Add the chopped mint and butter and stir together to mix well. Cook over a high heat, stirring, for 2 minutes. Serve immediately with couscous.

SERVES 4

Calories per serving 302
Preparation time 10 minutes
Cooking time 6–8 minutes

INGREDIENTS

1   12 sardines, cleaned and gutted

2   2 tablespoons harissa

3   chopped coriander, to garnish

STORECUPBOARD

2 tablespoons olive oil; juice of 1 lemon, plus lemon wedges, to serve; salt flakes and black pepper

Moroccan Grilled Sardines

■ Heat the grill on the hottest setting. Rinse the sardines and pat dry with kitchen paper. Make several deep slashes on both sides of each fish with a sharp knife.

■ Mix the harissa with the oil and lemon juice to make a thin paste. Rub into the sardines on both sides. Put the sardines on a lightly oiled baking sheet. Cook under the grill for 3–4 minutes on each side, depending on their size, or until cooked through. Season to taste with salt flakes and pepper and serve immediately garnished with coriander and with lemon wedges for squeezing over.

BAKE WITH PESTO

Line a medium ovenproof dish with 2 sliced tomatoes and 2 sliced onions. Prepare the sardines as for the main recipe, then rub 4 tablespoons pesto over the fish instead of the harissa paste and arrange in a single layer on top of the tomatoes and onions. Cover with foil and bake in a preheated oven, 200°C (400°F), Gas Mark 6, for 20–25 minutes or until the fish is cooked through. Calories per serving 375

SERVES 6

Calories per serving 148
Preparation time 20 minutes
Cooking time 4–7 minutes

INGREDIENTS

| 1 | 2 thick-cut sirloin steaks, about 500 g (1 lb) in total |

| 2 | 200 g (7 oz) natural yogurt |

| 3 | 1–1½ teaspoons horseradish sauce (to taste) |

| 4 | 150 g (5 oz) mixed green salad leaves |

| 5 | 100 g (3½ oz) button mushrooms, sliced |

STORECUPBOARD

3 teaspoons coloured peppercorns, coarsely crushed; coarse salt flakes; 1 garlic clove, crushed; 1 red onion, thinly sliced; 1 tablespoon olive oil salt and black pepper

Peppered Beef with Salad Leaves

■ Trim the fat from the steaks and rub the meat with the crushed peppercorns and salt flakes.

■ Mix together the yogurt, horseradish sauce and garlic and season to taste with salt and pepper. Add the salad leaves, mushrooms and most of the red onion and toss together gently.

■ Heat the oil in a frying pan, add the steaks and cook over a high heat for 2 minutes until browned. Turn over and cook for 2 minutes for medium rare, 3–4 minutes for medium or 5 minutes for well done.

■ Spoon the salad leaves into the centre of six serving plates. Thinly slice the steaks and arrange the pieces on top, then garnish with the remaining red onion.

SERVES 4

Calories per serving 475
Preparation time 12 minutes, plus marinating
Cooking time 8 minutes

INGREDIENTS

1 1 egg, lightly beaten

2 500 g (1 lb) boneless, skinless chicken breasts, cut into 5 mm (¼ inch) slices

3 1 spring onion, diagonally sliced into 1.5 cm (¾ inch) lengths

4 160 g (5½ oz) long-grain rice

STORECUPBOARD

2 garlic cloves, sliced; 2 small pieces of lemon rind, plus juice of 1 lemon; 2 tablespoons cornflour; 1 tablespoon rapeseed or olive oil; lemon slices, to garnish

Low-fat Lemon Chicken

■ Mix the egg, garlic and lemon rind together in a shallow dish, add the chicken and leave to marinate for 10–15 minutes.

■ Remove the lemon rind and add the cornflour to the marinated chicken. Mix thoroughly to distribute the cornflour evenly among the chicken slices.

■ Heat the oil in a wok over a high heat until the oil starts to shimmer. Add the chicken slices, making sure you leave a little space between them, and fry for 2 minutes on each side.

■ Reduce the heat to medium and stir-fry for 1 more minute or until the chicken is browned and cooked. Turn up the heat and pour in the lemon juice. Add the spring onion, garnish with lemon slices and serve immediately with boiled rice.

SERVES 4

Calories per serving 308 (excluding pasta)
Preparation time 10 minutes
Cooking time 10 minutes

INGREDIENTS

1	4 lamb leg steaks, about 125 g (4 oz) each, fat trimmed off
2	6 tablespoons chopped flat leaf parsley, plus extra whole sprigs to garnish
3	12 sun-dried tomatoes
4	2 tablespoons caperberries, rinsed

STORECUPBOARD

1 garlic clove, crushed; 1 tablespoon lemon juice; 1 tablespoon olive oil; salt and black pepper

Grilled Lamb with Caperberries

■ Season the meat and cook under a preheated hot grill for about 5 minutes on each side until golden.

■ Reserve 4 tablespoons of the chopped parsley. Blend the remaining parsley with the garlic, tomatoes, lemon juice and oil.

■ Spoon the tomato sauce over the lamb. Sprinkle over the reserved chopped flat leaf parsley and add the caperberries. Garnish with whole parsley sprigs and serve with pasta, if liked.

TRY A TAPENADE

Use black olive tapenade instead of the dressing and stir all the parsley through it. To make your own tapenade, whiz 150 g (5 oz) pitted black olives, 3 tablespoons extra virgin olive oil, 1 garlic clove and 2 salted anchovies in a food processor with black pepper and add chopped flat leaf parsley to taste. Calories per serving (with steak) 357

SERVES 2

Calories per serving 452
Preparation time 15 minutes
Cooking time 5 minutes

INGREDIENTS

1   10-12 prepared baby squid, about 375 g (12 oz) including tentacles, cleaned

2   2 red chillies, deseeded and finely chopped

3   2.5 cm (1 inch) piece of fresh root ginger, peeled and grated

4   100 g (3½ oz) freshly grated coconut

5   mixed salad leaves, to serve

STORECUPBOARD

4 lemons, halved, plus finely grated rind and juice of 2 lemons; 4 tablespoons groundnut oil; 1-2 tablespoons chilli oil; 1 tablespoon white wine vinegar

Coconut Citrus Squid

■ Cut down the side of each squid and lay flat on a chopping board. Using a sharp knife, lightly crisscross the inside flesh.

■ Mix the lemon juice, chillies, ginger, coconut, oils and vinegar together. Toss the squid in half the dressing until coated.

■ Heat a griddle pan until smoking hot, add the lemons, cut side down, and cook for 2 minutes until well charred. Remove from the pan and set aside. Keeping the griddle pan very hot, add the squid pieces and cook for 1 minute. Turn them over and cook for a further minute or until they turn white, lose their transparency and are charred.

■ Transfer the squid to a chopping board and cut into strips. Drizzle with the remaining dressing and serve immediately with the charred lemons and mixed salad leaves.

SOMETHING SWEET

SERVES 12

Calories per serving 282
Preparation time 1 minute
Cooking time 4 minutes

INGREDIENTS

1	120 g (4 oz) popping corn

2	250 g (8 oz) butter

3	2 tablespoons cocoa powder

STORECUPBOARD

250 g (8 oz) light muscovado sugar

Toffee & Chocolate Popcorn

■ Microwave the popping corn in a large bowl with a lid on high (900 watts) for 4 minutes. Alternatively, cook in a pan with a lid on the hob, on a medium heat, for a few minutes until popping.

■ Meanwhile, gently heat the butter, muscovado sugar and cocoa powder in a pan until the sugar has dissolved and the butter has melted.

■ Stir the warm popcorn into the mixture and serve.

MAKE IT CHEWY

Omit the muscovado sugar and cocoa. Microwave the popping corn as for the main recipe, then gently heat 150 g (5 oz) chewy toffees, 125 g (4 oz) butter, 125 g (4 oz) marshmallows and 50 g (2 oz) plain chocolate in a pan until melted. Serve as for the main recipe. Calories per serving 341

SERVES 4

Calories per serving 177
Preparation time 5 minutes

INGREDIENTS

| 1 | 300 g (10 oz) raspberries, roughly chopped |

| 2 | 4 shortbread fingers, roughly crushed |

| 3 | 400 g (13 oz) low-fat fromage frais |

STORECUPBOARD

2 tablespoons icing sugar or artificial sweetener

Raspberry Shortbread Mess

■ Reserving a few raspberries for decoration, combine all the ingredients in a bowl. Spoon into 4 serving dishes.

■ Serve immediately, decorated with the reserved raspberries.

MAKE AN ETON MESS

Use 4 meringue nests and 300 g (10 oz) strawberries. Hull and halve or quarter the strawberries, then add them to the fromage frais with the sugar or sweetener. Break the meringues into chunks and fold them through the fromage frais, then pile into glasses and serve. Calories per serving 143

SERVES 2

Calories per serving 131
Preparation time 10 minutes, plus chilling
Cooking time 1–2 minutes

INGREDIENTS

1	½ small mango, peeled, stoned and thinly sliced
2	1 passion fruit, halved and flesh scooped out
3	150 g (5 oz) low-fat natural yogurt
4	100 g (3½ oz) crème fraîche
5	a few drops of vanilla extract

STORECUPBOARD

½ tablespoon icing sugar; 1 tablespoon demerara sugar

Mango & Passion Fruit Brûlées

■ Divide the mango slices evenly between 2 ramekins.

■ Mix together the passion fruit flesh, yogurt, crème fraîche, icing sugar and vanilla essence in a bowl, then spoon the mixture over the mango. Tap each ramekin to level the surface.

■ Sprinkle over the demerara sugar, then cook the brûlées under a hot grill for 1–2 minutes until the sugar has melted. Chill for about 30 minutes before serving.

SERVES 4

Calories per serving 112
Preparation time 5 minutes, plus standing

INGREDIENTS

1	2 ripe bananas

2	15 g (½ oz) crystallized or glacé ginger, finely chopped, plus extra to decorate

3	150 g (5 oz) low-fat natural yogurt

STORECUPBOARD

juice of ½ lemon; 8 teaspoons dark muscovado sugar

Banana & Muscovado Ripples

■ Toss the bananas in a little lemon juice and mash on a plate with a fork. Add the ginger and yogurt and mix together. Spoon one-third of the mixture into the bases of 4 small dessert glasses.

■ Sprinkle 1 teaspoon of the sugar over each dessert. Spoon half of the remaining banana mixture on top, then repeat with a second layer of sugar. Complete the layers with the remaining banana mixture and decorate with a little extra ginger, cut into slightly larger pieces.

■ Leave the puddings to stand for 10–15 minutes for the sugar to dissolve and form a syrupy layer between the layers of banana yogurt. Serve immediately.

MAKES 9

Calories per serving 204
Preparation time 10 minutes
Cooking time 30 minutes

INGREDIENTS

1   125 g (4 oz) reduced-fat sunflower spread

2   2 eggs

3   50 g (2 oz) cocoa, sieved, plus extra to decorate

4   50 g (2 oz) plain dark chocolate, chopped

5   1 teaspoon chocolate extract

STORECUPBOARD

125 g (4 oz) light soft brown sugar; 75 g (3 oz) self-raising flour; salt

Chocolate Brownies

■ Grease and line an 18 cm (7 inch) square deep cake tin.

■ Beat together the sunflower spread, eggs and sugar. Stir in the flour and cocoa, then add the chocolate and chocolate extract. Stir in 1 teaspoon boiling water and a pinch of salt.

■ Transfer the mixture to the prepared tin and bake in a preheated oven, 190°C (375°F), Gas Mark 5, for 30 minutes or until a skewer comes out clean when inserted in the centre. Leave to cool in the tin then cut into 9 squares. Dust with a little cocoa powder to serve.

MAKES 24 SQUARES

Calories per serving 201
Preparation time 25 minutes, plus cooling
Cooking time 55 minutes

INGREDIENTS

1	200 g (7 oz) lightly salted butter, softened, plus extra for greasing
2	225 g (7½ oz) stoned dates, chopped
3	150 ml (¼ pint) double cream
4	2 teaspoons vanilla bean paste
5	3 eggs

STORECUPBOARD

150 ml (¼ pint) water; 175 g (6 oz) light muscovado sugar; 100 g (3½ oz) caster sugar; 175 g (6 oz) self-raising flour; ½ teaspoon baking powder

Sticky Toffee & Date Squares

■ Grease and line a 28 × 18 cm (11 × 7 inch) shallow baking tin with nonstick baking paper. Put 125 g (4 oz) of the dates in a saucepan with the water and bring to the boil. Reduce the heat and cook gently for 5 minutes or until the dates are pulpy. Turn into a bowl and leave to cool. Put the cream, muscovado sugar and 75 g (3 oz) of the butter in a small saucepan and heat gently until the sugar dissolves. Bring to the boil and boil for 5 minutes or until thickened and caramelized. Leave to cool.

■ Put the remaining butter in a bowl with the caster sugar, vanilla bean paste and eggs, sift in the flour and baking powder and beat with a hand-held electric whisk until pale and creamy. Beat in the cooked dates and 100 ml (3½ fl oz) of the caramel mixture. Turn into the tin and level the surface. Scatter with the remaining dates.

■ Bake in a preheated oven, 180°C (350°F), Gas Mark 4, for 25 minutes, or until just firm. Spoon the remaining caramel on top and return to the oven for 15 minutes until the caramel has firmed. Transfer to a wire rack to cool.

Calories per serving 240
Preparation time 10 minutes, plus chilling
Cooking time 3 minutes

INGREDIENTS

1   200 g (7 oz) milk chocolate, broken into pieces

2   2 tablespoons golden syrup

3   50 g (2 oz) olive oil spread, plus extra for greasing

4   125 g (4 oz) cornflakes

Chocolate Cornflake Bars

■ Melt the chocolate with the golden syrup and olive oil spread in a bowl over a pan of simmering water.

■ Stir in the cornflakes and mix everything well together.

■ Grease a 28 × 18 cm (11 × 7 inch) tin. Turn the mixture into the tin, chill until set, then cut into 12 bars.

MAKES 10

Calories per serving 345
Preparation time 25 minutes, plus proving
Cooking time 12–15 minutes

INGREDIENTS

1	1 tablespoon fast-action dried yeast
2	25 g (1 oz) slightly salted butter, melted
3	300 ml (½ pint) hand-hot milk, plus extra if required
4	2 teaspoons vanilla extract
5	pink food colouring

STORECUPBOARD

500 g (1 lb) strong white bread flour; 50 g (2 oz) caster sugar; 300 g (10 oz) fondant icing sugar

Simple Iced Buns

■ Mix together the flour, caster sugar and yeast in a bowl. Add the butter, milk and vanilla and mix to a fairly soft dough, adding a dash more milk or hot water if the dough feels dry. Knead the dough for 10 minutes on a floured surface until smooth and elastic. Put in a lightly oiled bowl, cover with clingfilm and leave to rise in a warm place for about 1 hour or until doubled in size.

■ Punch the dough to deflate it, then divide into 10 even-sized pieces on a floured surface and shape each into a sausage shape. Place, well spaced apart, on a large greased baking sheet. Cover loosely with greased clingfilm and leave to rise for 30 minutes.

■ Bake in a preheated oven, 200°C (400°F), Gas Mark 6, for 12–15 minutes until risen and pale golden (placing a roasting

tin filled with 1.5 cm (¾ inch) hot water on the lower shelf to prevent a firm crust forming). Transfer to a wire rack to cool.

■ Make the icing. Sift the icing sugar into a bowl and gradually beat in a little water, a teaspoonful at a time, to make a smooth, spreadable icing. Spread half over 5 of the buns. Add a dash of pink food colouring to the remaining icing and spread over the rest of the buns. Best eaten freshly baked.

MAKES ABOUT 30

Calories per serving 80
Preparation time 20 minutes, plus setting
Cooking time 30 minutes

INGREDIENTS

1 — 125 g (4 oz) lightly salted butter, melted, plus extra for greasing

2 — 2 teaspoons cardamom pods

3 — 3 eggs

STORECUPBOARD

125 g (4 oz) self-raising flour, plus extra for dusting; 125 g (4 oz) caster sugar; finely grated rind of 1 lemon, plus 2 tablespoons lemon juice; ½ teaspoon baking powder; 75 g (3 oz) icing sugar, sifted, plus extra for dusting

Lemon Glazed Cardamom Madeleines

■ Grease a madeleine tray with melted butter and dust with flour. Tap out the excess flour.

■ Crush the cardamom pods using a pestle and mortar to release the seeds. Remove the shells and crush the seeds a little further.

■ Put the eggs, caster sugar, lemon rind and crushed cardamom seeds in a heatproof bowl and rest the bowl over a saucepan of gently simmering water. Whisk with a hand-held electric whisk until the mixture is thick and pale and the mixture leaves a trail when lifted.

■ Sift the flour and baking powder into the bowl and gently fold in using a large metal spoon. Drizzle the melted butter around the edges of the mixture and fold the ingredients together to combine. Spoon the mixture into the madeleine sections until about two-thirds full. (Keep the remaining mixture for a second batch.)

■ Bake in a preheated oven, 220°C (425°F), Gas Mark 7, for about 10 minutes until risen and golden. Leave in the tray for 5 minutes, then transfer to a wire rack.

■ Make the glaze by putting the lemon juice in a bowl and beating in the icing sugar. Brush over the madeleines and leave to set. Make a second batch with the remaining batter. Serve lightly dusted with icing sugar.

SERVES 4

Calories per serving 168 (excluding biscuits)
Preparation time 10 minutes

INGREDIENTS

1	1 large mango, peeled, stoned and cut into chunks
2	750 g (1½ lb) fat-free natural yogurt
3	1-2 tablespoons agave nectar, to taste
4	1 vanilla pod, split in half lengthways
5	4 passion fruit, halved

Creamy Mango & Passion Fruit

■ Place the mango in a food processor or blender and blend to a purée.

■ Put the yogurt and agave nectar in a large bowl, scrape in the seeds from the vanilla pod and beat together. Gently fold in the mango purée and spoon into tall glasses or glass serving dishes.

■ Scoop the seeds from the passion fruit and spoon over the mango yogurt. Serve immediately with thin biscuits, if liked.

TRY BLACKCURRANTS

Purée 250 g (8 oz) blackcurrants
as for the main recipe and fold into
the yogurt with the agave nectar,
according to taste, and 1 teaspoon
almond essence. Spoon into tall,
glass serving dishes and scatter
with toasted almonds, to serve.
Calories per serving 143

Calories per serving 217
Preparation time 30 minutes
Cooking time 45–60 minutes

INGREDIENTS

1 | 3 egg whites

2 | 50 g (2 oz) shelled pistachio nuts, finely chopped

3 | 150 g (5 oz) plain dark chocolate, broken into pieces

4 | 150 ml (¼ pint) double cream

STORECUPBOARD

175 g (6 oz) caster sugar

Pistachio & Chocolate Meringues

■ Whisk the egg whites in a large clean bowl until stiff. Gradually whisk in the sugar, a teaspoonful at a time, until it has all been added. Whisk for a few minutes more until the meringue mixture is thick and glossy.

■ Fold in the pistachios then spoon heaped teaspoonfuls of the mixture into rough swirly mounds on 2 large baking sheets lined with nonstick baking paper.

■ Bake in a preheated oven, 110°C (225°F), Gas Mark ¼, for 45–60 minutes or until the meringues are firm and may be easily peeled off the paper. Leave to cool still on the paper.

■ Melt the chocolate in a heatproof bowl set over a saucepan of gently simmering water. Lift the meringues off the paper and dip their bases into the chocolate to coat. Return to the paper, tilted on their sides

and leave in a cool place until the chocolate has hardened.

■ To serve, whip the cream until it just holds its shape then use it to sandwich the meringues together in pairs. Arrange the pairs in paper cake cases, if liked, on a cake plate or stand. Eat on the day they are filled. (Left plain, the meringues will keep for 2–3 days.)

MAKES 20 SQUARES

Calories per serving 248
Preparation time 30 minutes
Cooking time 30–35 minutes

INGREDIENTS

1	1 large mango
2	4 tablespoons apricot jam
3	2 kiwi fruit, sliced
4	250 g (8 oz) soft margarine
5	4 eggs

STORECUPBOARD

grated rind and juice of 2 lemons; 125 g (4 oz) caster sugar; 125 g (4 oz) light muscovado sugar; 250 g (8 oz) self-raising flour

Mango & Kiwi Upside Down Cake

■ Cut a thick slice off each side of the mango to reveal the large flat central stone. Cut the flesh away from the stone then peel and slice.

■ Mix the apricot jam with the juice of 1 of the lemons then spoon into the base of an 18 × 28 cm (7 × 11 inch) roasting tin lined with nonstick baking paper. Arrange the mango and kiwi fruit randomly over the top.

■ Put the lemon rind and rest of the juice in a mixing bowl or a food processor, add the remaining ingredients and beat until smooth. Spoon over the top of the fruit and spread the surface level. Bake in a preheated oven, 180°C (350°F), Gas Mark 4, for 30–35 minutes until well risen, the cake is golden and springs back when gently pressed with a fingertip.

■ Leave to cool in the tin for 10 minutes then invert the tin on to a wire rack, remove the tin and lining paper and leave to cool completely. Cut into 20 pieces and serve warm. This is best eaten on the day it is made.

MAKES 14 SQUARES

Calories per serving 102
Preparation time 10 minutes, plus setting
Cooking time 5 minutes

INGREDIENTS

1 200 g (7 oz) marshmallows, halved

2 40 g (1½ oz) unsalted butter, diced

3 100 g (3½ oz) crisped rice cereal

4 pink sugar sprinkles, to decorate

Marshmallow Crackle Squares

■ Reserve 50 g (2 oz) of the white marshmallows. Put 25 g (1 oz) of the butter and the remaining marshmallows into a saucepan and heat very gently until melted. Remove from the heat and stir in the cereal until evenly coated.

■ Spoon the mixture into an 18 cm (7 inch) square shallow baking tin, greased and lined with baking parchment, and pack down firmly with the back of a lightly oiled spoon.

■ Place the remaining butter and reserved marshmallows in a small saucepan and heat gently until melted. Drizzle into the tin in lines, then scatter the sprinkles over the top. Leave in a cool place for 2 hours or until firm.

■ Turn the set mixture out of the tin on to a board, peel off the lining paper and cut into small squares.

SERVES 4

Calories per serving 220
Preparation time 5 minutes
Cooking time 8–10 minutes

INGREDIENTS

1	**4 bananas, unpeeled**
2	**8 tablespoons fat-free Greek yogurt**
3	**4 tablespoons oatmeal or fine porridge oats**
4	**125 g (4 oz) blueberries**
5	**runny honey, to serve**

Griddled Bananas with Blueberries

■ Heat a griddle pan over a medium-hot heat, add the bananas and griddle for 8–10 minutes, or until the skins are beginning to blacken, turning occasionally.

■ Transfer the bananas to serving dishes and, using a sharp knife, cut open lengthways. Spoon over the yogurt and sprinkle with the oatmeal or oats and blueberries. Serve immediately, drizzled with a little honey.

A DELICIOUS YOGURT

Mix ½ teaspoon ground ginger with the yogurt in a bowl. Sprinkle with 2–4 tablespoons soft dark brown sugar, according to taste, the oatmeal and 4 tablespoons sultanas. Leave to stand for 5 minutes before serving. Calories per serving 208

MAKES 10 SLICES

Calories per serving 373
Preparation time 20 minutes, plus cooling
Cooking time 1 hour 25 minutes

INGREDIENTS

1	250 g (8 oz) stoned dates, roughly chopped
2	2 small very ripe bananas
3	150 g (5 oz) slightly salted butter, softened
4	2 eggs
5	100 ml (3½ fl oz) milk

STORECUPBOARD

finely grated rind and juice of 1 lemon; 100 ml (3½ fl oz) water; 150 g (5 oz) caster sugar; 275 g (9 oz) self-raising flour; 1 teaspoon baking powder

Date & Banana Ripple Slice

■ Put 200 g (7 oz) of the dates in a small saucepan with the lemon rind and juice and measurement water. Bring to the boil, then reduce the heat and simmer gently for 5 minutes until the dates are soft and pulpy. Mash the mixture with a fork until fairly smooth. Leave to cool.

■ Mash the bananas to a purée in a bowl, then add the butter, sugar, eggs, milk, flour and baking powder and beat together until the mixture is smooth.

■ Spoon a third of the mixture into a greased and lined 1.25 kg (2½ lb) or 1.5 litre (2½ pint) loaf tin and level the surface. Spoon over half the date purée and spread evenly. Add half the remaining cake mixture and spread with the remaining purée. Add the remaining cake mixture and level the surface.

■ Scatter with the reserved dates and bake in a preheated oven, 160°C (325°F), Gas Mark 3, for about 1 hour 20 minutes or until risen and a skewer inserted into the centre comes out clean. Cool in the tin for 15 minutes, then loosen around the sides and transfer to a wire rack. Peel off the lining paper and leave the cake to cool completely.

SERVES 6

Calories per serving 216
Preparation time 30 minutes, plus freezing
Cooking time 2–4 minutes

INGREDIENTS

1 425 g (14 oz) can pitted lychees in light syrup

2 400 ml (14 fl oz) can full-fat coconut milk

3 grated rind and juice of 1 lime, plus extra pared lime rind, to decorate (optional)

4 3 kiwi fruit, peeled and cut into wedges, to decorate

STORECUPBOARD

50 g (2 oz) caster sugar

Lychee & Coconut Sherbet

■ Drain the syrup from the can of lychees into a saucepan, add the sugar and heat gently until the sugar has dissolved. Boil for 2 minutes, then take off the heat and leave to cool.

■ Purée the lychees in a food processor or liquidizer until smooth, or rub through a sieve. Mix with the coconut milk, lime rind and juice. Stir in the sugar syrup when it is cool.

■ Pour into a shallow plastic container and freeze for 4 hours or until mushy. Beat with a fork or blend in a food processor or liquidizer until smooth. Pour back into the plastic container and freeze for 4 hours or overnight until solid. (Alternatively, freeze in an electric ice-cream machine for 20 minutes, then transfer to a plastic box and freeze until required.)

■ Allow to soften for 15 minutes at room temperature before serving, then scoop into dishes (or chocolate cups if preferred, see right) and decorate with kiwi fruit wedges and pared lime rind curls, if liked.

SERVE IN CHOCOLATE CUPS

For chocolate cups, to serve
the sherbet in, melt 150 g (5 oz)
plain dark chocolate over a pan
of simmering water, then divide
between 4 squares of nonstick
baking paper and spread into
rough-shaped circles about 15 cm
(6 inches) in diameter. Drape the
paper over upturned glass tumblers,
with the chocolate uppermost, so
that the paper falls in soft folds.
Chill until set, then lift the paper
and chocolate off the tumblers, turn
over and carefully ease the paper
away. Calories per serving 195

Calories per serving 327
Preparation time 1 minute
Cooking time 4 minutes

INGREDIENTS

| 1 | 300 g (10 oz) plain dark chocolate |

| 2 | 500 g (1 lb) fat-free fromage frais |

| 3 | 1 teaspoon vanilla extract |

Warm Chocolate Fromage frais

■ Melt the chocolate in a heatproof bowl set over a pan of simmering water, then remove from the heat.

■ Add the fromage frais and vanilla extract and quickly stir together.

■ Divide the chocolate fromage frais among 6 little pots or glasses and serve immediately.

MAKE IT CAPPUCCINO

Melt the plain dark chocolate with 2 tablespoons very strong espresso coffee. Divide among 6 espresso cups, finishing each with 1 teaspoon regular fromage frais and a dusting of cocoa powder. Calories per serving 339

INDEX

PICTURE CREDITS